Feel-Bad Education

Feel-Bad Education

And Other Contrarian Essays on Children and Schooling

Alfie Kohn

Beacon Press, Boston

BEACON PRESS
25 Beacon Street
Boston, Massachusetts 02108–2892
www.beacon.org

Beacon Press books
are published under the auspices of
the Unitarian Universalist Association of Congregations.

14 13 12 11   8 7 6 5 4 3 2 1

This book is printed on acid-free paper that meets the uncoated paper
ANSI/NISO specifications for permanence as revised in 1992.

Text design and composition by Wilsted & Taylor Publishing Services

Library of Congress Cataloging-in-Publication Data
Kohn, Alfie.
  Feel-bad education : and other contrarian essays on children and schooling / Alfie Kohn.
    p. cm.
  Includes bibliographical references and index.
  ISBN 978-0-8070-0140-0 (pbk. : alk. paper)
    1. Public schools—United States. 2. Education—Aims and objectives—United States.
I. Title.
  LA217.2.K64 2011
  370.973—dc22   2010037081

To the memory—and enduring legacy—of two thinkers who have influenced so many of us: Ted Sizer (1932–2009) and Jerry Bracey (1940–2009)

Contents

Five: Beyond the Schools: Psychological Issues & Parenting

Introduction
"Well, Duh!": Obvious Truths That We Shouldn't Be Ignoring

The field of education bubbles over with controversies. It's not unusual for intelligent people of good will to disagree passionately about what should happen in schools. Sometimes these disagreements result from how the available evidence is interpreted, and sometimes they're due to divergent visions regarding the purpose of schooling or what constitutes an ideal society.

But there are certain precepts that aren't really debatable—that just about anyone would have to acknowledge are true. While many such statements are banal, I want to argue that some are worth noticing, because in our school practices and policies, we tend to ignore the implications that follow from them. It's both intellectually interesting and practically important to explore such contradictions: *If we all agree that a given principle is true, then why in the world do our schools still function as if it weren't?* I'll identify about a dozen examples of this phenomenon, mindful that it won't be possible to explore all the specific issues—and more controversial implications—that are entangled within them. Not so coincidentally, many of these questions anticipate the very topics that are explored later in this book.

I should also mention that several thinkers whose work I admire were kind enough to add to my "duh" list. I wasn't able to use all their suggestions, but many stimulated my thinking about the items that I did include and helped me to reframe them.[1] In any case, the hazard of creating such a list is that "Duh" will inevitably become "D'oh!" as more examples come to mind immediately after it's sent off to the printer. You, meanwhile, will undoubtedly think of still others, some of which may be even more obvious.

1. Much of the material that students are required to memorize is soon forgotten. The truth of this statement will be conceded (either willingly or reluctantly) by just about everyone who has spent time in school—in other words, all of us. A few months, or sometimes even just a few days, after having committed a list of facts, dates, or definitions to memory, we couldn't recall most of them if our lives depended on it.

Everyone knows this, yet a substantial part of schooling—particularly in the most traditional schools—continues to consist of stuffing facts into students' short-term memories. Instruction and assessment are largely geared to "the forced ingestion of facts and data," even though this is "useless for educational purposes," as literacy expert Frank Smith has written. "What we remember from fruitless efforts to memorize are the stress and the failure inevitably involved."[2]

The more closely we inspect this model of teaching and testing, the more problematic it reveals itself to be. First, there's the question of *what* students are made to learn, which often is more oriented to factual material than to a deep understanding of ideas. (For more on this, see item #2 below.) Second, there's the question of *how* students are taught, with a focus on passive absorption rather than active meaning-making: listening to lectures, reading predigested summaries in textbooks, and rehearsing material immediately before being required to cough it back up. Third, there's the question of *why* a student has learned something: Knowledge is less likely to be retained if it has been acquired so that one will perform well on a test, as opposed to learning in the context of pursuing projects and solving problems that are personally meaningful.

Even without these layers of deficiencies with the status quo, and even if we grant that remembering some things can be useful, the fundamental question echoes like a shout down an endless school corridor: Why are kids still being forced to memorize so much stuff that we know they won't remember?

Corollary 1a: Because this appears to be true for adults, too, why do most "professional development" events for teachers resemble the least impressive classrooms, with experts disgorging facts about how to educate?

2. Just knowing a lot of facts doesn't mean that one is smart.
Even students who do manage to remember some of the factual material that they were taught are not necessarily able to make sense of those bits of knowledge, to understand connections among them, or to apply them in inventive and persuasive ways to real-life problems. To cite an old adage (which was also cited approvingly by Albert Einstein): "Education is that which remains if one has forgotten everything he learned in school."[3] Words like "smart" and "intelligent" are routinely used to describe people who merely know a lot of facts, yet I think most people will admit that there's a difference.

In fact, the cognitive scientist Lauren Resnick goes even further: It's not just that knowing (or having been taught) facts doesn't in itself make you smart. A mostly fact-oriented education may actually *interfere* with your becoming smart. "Thinking skills tend to be driven out of the curriculum by ever-growing demands for teaching larger and larger bodies of knowledge," she writes.[4] Yet schools continue to treat students as empty glasses into which information can be poured—and public officials continue to judge schools on the basis of how efficiently and determinedly they pour.

3. If kids have different talents, interests, and ways of learning, it's probably not ideal to teach all of them the same things—or in the same way. It's tempting to assume that one-size-fits-all instruction persists only because there are too many students in each classroom for teachers to customize what, or how, they're teaching. This explanation, however, doesn't quite match reality.

First, some teachers manage to adjust the curriculum to the needs of each student quite effectively despite class sizes far greater than would be ideal.[5] Second, many people seem to value uniformity and consistency in teaching—or overlook the significance of differences among students—to the point that a lockstep curriculum and a single set of (usually traditional) teaching strategies are used even when this is avoidable. Lots of teachers will do pretty much the same thing next year that they did this year, even though they're teaching different students. Many schools insist on "aligning" the curriculum so that what's being taught in all the fifth-grade classrooms is virtually identical. (The degree of predictability that this arrangement ensures is convenient for the sixth-grade teachers who will inherit these kids, but why should that consideration trump what's best for the kids themselves?) Finally, policy makers mandate a uniform set of standards and curriculum topics for all students of the same age across a district, across a state, and now, it appears, throughout the entire country (see chapter 15, "Debunking the Case for National Standards"). Most of us understand on some level that one size is more likely to thwart than to fit all, yet education policies proceed as if that weren't the case.

4. Students are more likely to learn what they find interesting. There's no shortage of evidence for this claim if you really need it. One of many examples: A group of researchers found that children's level of interest in a passage they were reading was *thirty times* more useful than its difficulty level for predicting how much of it they would later remember.[6] But this should be obvious, if only because of what we know about ourselves. It's the tasks that intrigue us, that tap our curiosity and connect to the things we care about, that we tend to keep doing—and get better at doing. So, too, for kids.

Conversely, students are less likely to benefit from doing what they hate. Medicine may work on the body regardless of your attitude about taking it,[7] but that's not true with education. Psychology has come a long way from the days when theorists tried to reduce everything to simple stimulus-response pairings. We know now that people aren't machines, such that an input (listening to a lecture, reading a textbook, filling out a worksheet) will reliably yield an output (learning). What matters is how people *experience* what they do, what meaning they ascribe to it, and what their attitudes and goals are. Thus, if students find an academic task stressful or boring, they're far less likely to understand, or even remember, the content. And if they're uninterested in a whole category of academic tasks— say, those that they're assigned to do when they get home after having spent a whole day at school—then they aren't likely to benefit much from doing them. No wonder research finds little, if any, advantage to homework, particularly in elementary or middle school.[8]

Sure, some things have to be done even though they're not much fun. But quality of life improves when people of any age have more opportunities to do what they find interesting, and so does their productivity. So why does students' level of interest in what they're doing have so little impact on education policy despite its obvious connection to achievement?

Corollary 4a: If a certain approach to teaching left most of *us* bored and unenlightened, we probably shouldn't teach another generation the same way. As far as I can tell, the vast majority of adults were themselves children at one point or another. So why do educators subject kids—and why do parents allow their kids to be subjected—to the stuff that we found barely tolerable? Have we forgotten what it was like? Or do we, for lack of empathy, regard the lectures, worksheets, tests, grades, and homework as a rite of passage?

5. Students are less interested in whatever they're forced to do and more enthusiastic when they have some say. Once again, it's true for you, it's true for me, it's true for people who spend their days in classrooms and in workplaces. Once again, studies confirm what we already know from experience (see chapter 6, "How to Create Nonreaders"). The nearly universal negative reaction to compulsion, like the positive response to choice, is a function of our psychological makeup.

Now combine this point with the preceding one: If choice is related to interest, and interest is related to achievement, then it's not much of a stretch to suggest that the learning environments in which kids get to participate in making decisions about what they're doing are likely to be the most effective, all else being equal. Yet such learning environments continue to be vastly outnumbered by those where kids spend most of their time just following directions.

6. Just because doing X raises standardized test scores doesn't mean X should be done. At the very least, we would need evidence that the test in question is a source of useful information about whether our teaching and learning goals are being met. Many educators have argued that the tests being used in our schools are unsatisfactory because of (a) limitations with specific tests; (b) features shared by *most* tests, such as the fact that they're timed (which places more of a premium on speed than on thoughtfulness), norm-referenced (which means the tests are designed to tell us who's beating whom, not how well students have learned or teachers have taught), and consist largely of multiple-choice questions (which don't permit students to generate or even explain their answers); or (c) problems inherent to *all* tests that are standardized and created by people far away from the classroom, as opposed to assessing the actual learning taking place there on an ongoing basis.

This is not the place to explain in detail why standardized tests measure what matters least.[9] Here, I want only to make the simpler—and, once again, I think, indisputable—point that anyone who regards high or rising test scores as good news has an obligation to show that the tests themselves are good—in other words, that they really tap the proficiencies we care about, that students and schools we admire based on solid criteria also do well on these tests, and that when one school's score is higher than another's, we're certain that the difference is both statistically and practically significant (and can't be explained by other variables such as socioeconomic status).

If a test result *can't* be convincingly shown to be both valid and meaningful, then whatever we did to achieve that result—say, a new curriculum or instructional strategy—may well have no merit whatsoever. It may even prove to be destructive when assessed by better criteria. Indeed, a school might be getting worse even as its test scores rise.

So how is it that articles in newspapers and education journals, as well as pronouncements by public officials and think tanks, seem to accept on faith that better scores on *any* test necessarily constitute good news, and that whatever produced those scores can be described as "effective"? Flip through any issue of *Education Week* and you will see multiple illustrations: This reading program has produced "promising results"; that state has experienced stagnant "achievement"; certain school districts are "outperforming" others—and in every single case, the people being quoted (and those doing the quoting) are relying on the validity of the standardized tests on which these evaluations are based, almost never pausing to question, defend, or even acknowledge the significance of this reliance.

Corollary 6a: The more time spent teaching students how to do well on a particular test—familiarizing them with its content and format—the less meaningful the results of that test. What those results mostly tell us is how well students were prepared for *that test*, not what knowledge and skills they have in general. (The scores may not even predict how well students will do on other, apparently similar, standardized tests.) Every expert in the field of educational measurement knows this is true, yet administrators continue to encourage, if not demand, a test-oriented curriculum. Astute parents and other observers will then ask, "How much time was sacrificed from real learning just so kids could get better at taking the [name of test]?"

7. Students are more likely to succeed in a place where they feel known and cared about. I realize that there are people whose impulse is to sneer when talk turns to how kids feel, and who dismiss as "soft" or "faddish" anything other than old-fashioned instruction of academic skills. But even these hard-liners, when pressed, are unable to deny the relationship between feeling and thinking, between a child's comfort level and his or her capacity to learn.

Here, too, there are loads of supporting data. As one group of researchers put it, "In order to promote students' academic performance in the classroom, educators should also promote their social and emotional adjustment."[10] And yet, broadly speaking, we don't. Teachers and schools are evaluated almost exclusively on academic achievement measures (which, to make matters worse, mostly amount to standardized test scores). If we took seriously the need for kids to feel known and cared about, our discussions about the distinguishing features of a "good school" would sound very different, and our view of discipline and classroom management would be turned inside out, seeing as how the primary goals of most such strategies are obedience and order, often with the result that kids feel *less* cared about by adults—or even bullied by them.

Corollary 7a: Students are more likely to succeed when they're healthy and well-fed. Fourteen million American children live in families whose income falls below the official poverty line, and another 16 million live in families classified as low-income.[11] Can anyone possibly doubt the impact that hunger and inadequate health care have on academic achievement?[12] Is there a more striking example of the disparity between what we know and what we do?

8. We want children to develop in many ways, not just academically. Even mainstream education groups, averse to challenging widely accepted premises about instruction and assessment, have embraced the idea of teaching the "whole child." It's a safe position, really, because just about every parent or educator will tell you that we should be supporting children's physical, emotional, social, moral, and artistic growth, as well as their intellectual growth.[13] Moreover, it's obvious to most people that the schools can and should play a key role in promoting many different forms of development. In a survey of more than 1,100 Americans, for example, 71 percent said they thought that it was even more important for the schools to teach values than to teach academic subjects[14]—although of course this doesn't mean that everyone will agree on what those values should be.

If we acknowledge that academics is just one facet of a good education, why do so few conversations about improving our schools deal with—and why are so few resources devoted to—nonacademic issues? And why do we assign children still more academic tasks after the school day is over, even when those tasks cut into the time that children have to pursue interests that will help them develop in other ways?

Corollary 8a: Students "learn best when they are happy,"[15] but that doesn't mean they're especially likely to be happy (or psychologically healthy) just because they're academically successful. And millions aren't. Imagine how high schools would have to be changed if we were to take this realization seriously.

9. Just because a lesson (or book, or class, or test) is harder doesn't mean it's better. First, if it's pointless to give students things to do that are too easy, it's also counterproductive to give them things that they experience as too hard. Second, and more important, this criterion overlooks a variety of considerations other than difficulty level by which educational quality might be evaluated. We know this, yet we continue to worship at the altar of "rigor." I've seen lessons that aren't unduly challenging yet are deeply engaging and intellectually valuable. Conversely, I've seen courses—and whole schools—that are indisputably rigorous . . . and appallingly bad.[16]

Of course, difficulty level can be seen not only as a cause but also as an effect. And that leads us to . . .

Corollary 9a: The more pressure students feel to succeed, the more likely they'll be to choose easy tasks. After all, the easier the task, the higher the probability that it can be done successfully. The paradox is profound: Some of the same people who love to talk about "rigor" and "raising the bar" have created schools that are all about succeeding, performing, achieving (rather than *learning*), and that very focus leads students to do whatever's easiest.[17]

10. Kids aren't just short adults. Over the last hundred years, developmental psychologists have labored to describe what makes children distinctive and what they can understand at certain ages. There are limits, after all, to what even a precocious younger child can grasp (e.g., the way metaphors function, the significance of making a promise) or do (e.g., keep still for an extended period). Likewise, there are certain things children require for optimal development, including opportunities to play and explore, alone and with others. Research fills in—and keeps fine-tuning—the details, but the fundamental implication isn't hard to grasp: How we educate kids should follow from what defines them *as* kids.

Once again, though, our practices and policies deviate alarmingly from what most people acknowledge to be true in the abstract. Developmentally inappropriate education has become the norm, as kindergarten (literally, the "children's garden") now tends to resemble a first- or second-grade classroom—in fact, a *bad* first- or second-grade classroom, where discovery, creativity, and social interaction are replaced by a repetitive regimen focused on narrowly defined academic skills.

More generally, premature exposure to sit-still-and-listen instruction, homework, grades, tests, and competition—practices that are clearly a bad match for younger children and of questionable value at any age—is rationalized by invoking a notion I've called BGUTI: Better Get Used to It. The logic here is that we have to prepare you for the bad things that are going to be done to you later . . . by doing them to you now (see chapter 3, "Getting Hit on the Head Lessons"). When articulated explicitly, that principle sounds exactly as ridiculous as it is. Nevertheless, it's the engine that continues to drive an awful lot of nonsense.

The deeply obvious premise that we should respect what makes children children can be amended to include a related principle that is less obvious to some people: Learning something earlier isn't necessarily better. Deborah Meier, whose experience as a celebrated educator ranges from kindergarten to high school, put it bluntly: "The earlier [that schools try] to inculcate so-called 'academic' skills, the deeper the damage and the more permanent the 'achievement' gap."[18] That is exactly what a passel of ambitious research projects has found: A traditional skills-based approach to teaching young children—particularly those from low-income families—not only offers no lasting benefits but appears to be harmful.[19]

Another kind of evidence comes from Finland, whose impressive results on international comparisons in several academic fields have lately attracted intense interest. Most of what's striking about that country's education policy poses a direct challenge to the conventional wisdom that defines U.S. schooling: Standardized tests are used sparingly, students of different ability levels are taught together rather than tracked, and homework is uncommon. Any of these features might be contributing to Finland's success.[20] But it's particularly interesting that kids there don't start school until they're seven years old, and preschool begins only one year before that. During that preschool year, moreover, "children are encouraged to play with language and numbers," but "there is no formal teaching of basic academic skills."[21] From all indications, Finland succeeds because of, not in spite of, that fact.

Corollary 10a: Kids aren't just *future* adults. They are that, of course, but they aren't only that, because children's needs and perspectives are worth attending to in their own right. We violate this precept—and do a disservice to children—whenever we talk about schooling in economic terms, treating students mostly as future employees (see chapter 13, "Against 'Competitiveness'"). Which reminds us of another unarguable fact. . . .

11. Education policies that benefit (or appeal to) large corporations aren't necessarily good for children. I say "aren't necessarily" to ensure that this item qualifies for a place on the "duh" list. Replace that phrase with "often aren't" and I believe the claim is still true, even though it would then be contestable. Some years ago I made an observation so obvious that it should have been prefaced with the phrase "needless to say," but current developments in U.S. education reform suggest that it needs to be said again:

> Corporations in our economic system exist to provide a financial return to the people who own them: They are in business to make a profit. As individuals, those who work in (or even run) these companies might have other goals, too, when they turn their attention to public policy or education or anything else. But business *qua* business is concerned principally about its own bottom line. Thus, when business thinks about schools, its agenda is driven by what will maximize its profitability, not necessarily by what is in the best interest of students. Any overlap between those two goals would be purely accidental—and, in practice, turns out to be minimal. What maximizes corporate profits often does not benefit children, and vice versa. Qualities such as a love of learning for its own sake, a penchant for asking challenging questions, or a commitment to democratic participation in decision making would be seen as nice but irrelevant—or perhaps even as impediments to the efficient realization of corporate goals.[22]

To say this is not in itself to criticize those corporate goals, but merely to observe that the people who pursue them should not enjoy a privileged status when it comes to formulating education policy.

12. Substance matters more than labels. A skunk cabbage by any other name would smell as putrid. But in education, as in other domains, we're often seduced by appealing names when we should be demanding to know exactly what lies behind them. Most of us, for example, favor a sense of community, prefer that a job be done by professionals, and want to promote learning. So should we sign on to the work being done in the name of "Professional Learning Communities"? Not if it turns out that PLCs have less to do with helping children to think deeply about questions that matter than with boosting standardized test scores.[23] The same caution is appropriate when it comes to "Positive Behavior Support," a jaunty moniker for a program of crude Skinnerian manipulation in which students are essentially bribed to do whatever they're told. More broadly, even the label "school reform" doesn't necessarily signify improvement; these days, it's more likely to mean "something that skillful and caring teachers wouldn't be inclined to do unless coerced," as educator Bruce Marlowe put it.[24]

Corollary 12a: What it is matters more than when it's done. Just about anything that one happens to like can be rebranded as "twenty-first-century schooling" (or skills). It's sort of like "new and improved" except that what's being sold are books, conferences, and ideas rather than dessert toppings or floor waxes. Take the educational stuff that you regard as truly valuable—student-centered learning, critical thinking, understanding ideas from the inside out, compassion, collaboration, democracy, authentic assessment—and then ask whether any of it was (or will be) less important in a different century. When modifiers turn out to be mostly marketing ploys, it's enough to drive one to an act of satire (see chapter 14, "When Twenty-First-Century Schooling Just Isn't Good Enough").

Once we acknowledge that any given item on this list is true, we're compelled to consider its implications for both big-picture (macro) policies and little-picture (micro) practices. While the two obviously overlap—a state law that imposes high-stakes testing affects what Ms. Dewey can do tomorrow morning with her sixth graders—I've noticed that some people seem to make a lot more sense when they talk about one realm as opposed to the other.

For instance, certain scholars of cognition and pedagogy who demonstrate a keen sense of what can be done in classrooms to help children learn have enthusiastically endorsed the idea of prescriptive state (or even national) standards. Their assumption seems to be that the best and brightest theorists, using government as their instrument, ought to reach into classrooms and *make* the instruction more thoughtful. I find this at once naive and arrogant, troubling for moral as well as practical reasons. Some of these thinkers have contributed significantly to our understanding of the limits of a behaviorist model of learning—and the importance of having students construct knowledge rather than passively absorb it—but they assume that teachers' behaviors can (and should) be controlled from above, that public policy ought to be based on a model of "doing to" rather than "working with."

Conversely, consider the case of Diane Ravitch, a prominent conservative education scholar, who has undergone a conversion experience and begun to write trenchant critiques of the corporate-style version of education reform that many of us have been decrying for years: merit pay (mostly based on test results), more charter schools (which often siphon public funds to for-profit companies), less job security for teachers, and so on. But when the conversation turns to what happens *inside* classrooms, she remains steadfastly traditional. By way of analogy, imagine a health care critic who cheers progressives with her brilliant arguments for a single-payer plan and fiery, if belated, attacks on insurance companies—but, if asked what doctors should actually be doing in the examining room, waxes nostalgic for the curative value of leeches.

The essays that follow reflect what could be described as a progressive sensibility that applies to both macro and micro questions. I make a case against uniform national standards but also against the use of rubrics for evaluating kids' individual assignments; I object to using "competitiveness in a global economy" as the touchstone for formulating education policies, but I'm just as concerned about simplistic attempts to crack down on student cheating or the ideology that lies behind inspirational posters of the sort found in so many schools.

These and other positions developed in the chapters that you're about to read are obviously controversial. Yet I remain convinced that most of them, whether addressed to policy makers or teachers, derive from much more basic and widely accepted beliefs—in some cases from assertions so straightforward as to make us say, "Well, duh!"

Notes

1. Thanks to Dick Allington, David Berliner, Marion Brady, Bruce Marlowe, Ed Miller, Nel Noddings, Susan Ohanian, Richard Rothstein, and Eric Schaps.

2. Frank Smith, "Let's Declare Education a Disaster and Get On with Our Lives," *Phi Delta Kappan*, April 1995, p. 589.

3. Albert Einstein, *Out of My Later Years* (Secaucus, NJ: Citadel Press, 2000, orig. published 1950), p. 36.

4. Lauren B. Resnick, *Education and Learning to Think* (Washington, D.C.: National Academy Press, 1987), p. 48. The psychoanalyst Erich Fromm put it this way: "The pathetic superstition prevails that by knowing more and more facts, one arrives at knowledge of reality. Hundreds of scattered and unrelated facts are dumped into the heads of students; their time and energy are taken up by learning more and more facts so that there is little left for thinking" (*Escape from Freedom* [New York: Avon Books, 1965, orig. published 1946], p. 273).

5. The usual term for this is "differentiation," but it's important to distinguish between, on the one hand, a commitment to working with students individually to create projects that reflect their interests, strengths, and needs, and, on the other hand, a behaviorist protocol in which the difficulty level of prefabricated skills-based exercises is adjusted on the basis of each student's proficiency as determined by standardized test scores.

6. Richard C. Anderson et al., "Interestingness of Children's Reading Material," in *Aptitude, Learning, and Instruction,* vol. 3: *Conative and Affective*

Process Analyses, eds. Richard E. Snow and Marshall J. Farr (Hillsdale, NJ: Erlbaum, 1987).

7. For the sake of argument, we'll ignore some intriguing findings from the field of mind-body connections that have the effect of raising questions about even this assumption.

8. See Alfie Kohn, *The Homework Myth* (Cambridge, MA: Da Capo, 2006), especially chapters 2 and 3.

9. *This* is the place: Alfie Kohn, *The Case Against Standardized Testing: Raising the Scores, Ruining the Schools* (Portsmouth, NH: Heinemann, 2000). For a list of books on the subject by other authors, see www.alfiekohn.org/standards/resources.htm. Also see the resources at www.fairtest.org.

10. Lisa Flook, Rena L. Repetti, and Jodie B. Ullman, "Classroom Social Experiences as Predictors of Academic Performance," *Developmental Psychology* 41 (2005): 326. This particular study focused on the academic relevance of peer acceptance and social relations, but other research has found similar academic benefits from a feeling of "classroom belonging," which includes being accepted by the teacher (Carol Goodenow, "Classroom Belonging Among Early Adolescent Students: Relationships to Motivation and Achievement," *Journal of Early Adolescence* 13 [1993]: 21–43); the extent to which a classroom or school feels to students like a "community" (Victor Battistich et al., "Schools as Communities, Poverty Levels of Student Populations, and Students' Attitudes, Motives, and Performance," *American Educational Research Journal* 32 [1995]: 627–58); and attending to students' social and emotional needs more generally (Joseph E. Zins et al., eds., *Building Academic Success on Social and Emotional Learning: What Does the Research Say?* [New York: Teachers College Press, 2004]; and Catherine Gewertz, "Hand in Hand," *Education Week,* September 3, 2003, pp. 38–41). At the same time, it's important to keep in mind that caring, like the chance to make decisions and to do interesting things, is an end in itself, not merely a means of boosting academic performance.

11. See publications by the National Center for Children in Poverty (www.nccp .org).

12. For a good summary, see Richard Rothstein, "Equalizing Opportunity," *American Educator,* Summer 2009, pp. 4–7, 45–46. Elsewhere, Rothstein suggests that schools might raise achievement more by making sure children had access to dental and vision clinics than from changing instruction ("Reforms That Could Help Narrow the Achievement Gap," *Policy Perspectives,* p. 5; available at www.wested.org/online_pubs/pp-06-02.pdf).

13. What's more, even a desire to promote *intellectual* growth doesn't necessarily translate into support for what we commonly think of as an *academic*

agenda. In many of her writings, early-childhood expert Lilian Katz has distinguished between engaging children's minds and deepening their understanding of themselves, on the one hand, and the more circumscribed skills associated with a focus on academic achievement, on the other.

14. Jean Johnson and John Immerwahr, *First Things First: What Americans Expect from Public Schools* (New York: Public Agenda, 1994). In a Phi Delta Kappa/Gallup poll with about the same sample size, meanwhile, when respondents were asked what "the local public schools should give the main emphasis to," 39 percent chose "academic skills of students," while 59 percent chose one of the other two options: "ability of students to take responsibility" or "ability of students to work with others" (Lowell C. Rose and Alec M. Gallup, "The 31st Annual Phi Delta Kappa/Gallup Poll of the Public's Attitudes Toward the Public Schools," *Phi Delta Kappan*, September 1999, p. 51).

15. This reminder from education philosopher Nel Noddings is quoted in chapter 12 of this book ("Feel-Bad Education").

16. For more on this topic, see my article "Confusing Harder with Better," *Education Week*, September 15, 1999, pp. 68, 52, which appears as a chapter in *What Does It Mean to Be Well Educated?* (Boston: Beacon Press, 2004) and is available at www.alfiekohn.org/teaching/edweek/chwb.htm.

17. For more, see my book *The Schools Our Children Deserve* (Boston: Houghton Mifflin, 1999), chapter 2.

18. Deborah Meier, "What I've Learned," in *Those Who Dared*, ed. Carl Glickman (New York: Teachers College Press, 2009), p. 12.

19. One study, for example, found that young children subjected to "Direct Instruction" (DI) were subsequently less likely to graduate from high school than those who experienced a more developmentally appropriate form of teaching. Another study found that DI children ended up with more social and psychological signs of trouble later on and were less likely to read books. See Kohn, *The Schools Our Children Deserve*, pp. 213–17. This section is also available at www.alfiekohn.org/teaching/ece.htm.

20. Also possibly relevant: the fact that Finland is a small, mostly homogeneous country with egalitarian sensibilities and an institutionalized respect for teachers.

21. Kaisa Aunola and Jari-Erik Nurmi, "Maternal Affection Moderates the Impact of Psychological Control on a Child's Mathematical Performance," *Developmental Psychology* 40 (2004): 968. Also see Ellen Gamerman, "What Makes Finnish Kids So Smart?" *Wall Street Journal*, February 29, 2008 (available at http://online.wsj.com/article/SB120425355065601997.html).

22. Alfie Kohn, "The 500-Pound Gorilla," *Phi Delta Kappan*, October 2002, p. 118 (available at www.alfiekohn.org/teaching/500pound.htm).

23. For more, see my essay "Turning Children into Data: A Skeptic's Guide to Assessment Programs," *Education Week*, August 25, 2010 (available at www .alfiekohn.org/teaching/edweek/data.htm).

24. Bruce Marlowe, personal communication, May 2010. Also see my comments on the uses to which the phrase "school reform" is put, in "Test Today, Privatize Tomorrow," *Phi Delta Kappan*, April 2004, pp. 569–77 (available at www.alfiekohn.org/teaching/testtoday.htm); and in "Beware School 'Reformers,'" *Nation*, December 29, 2008, pp. 7–8 (available at www.alfiekohn .org/teaching/soe.htm).

One: Progressivism and Beyond

1. Progressive Education: Why It's Hard to Beat, But Also Hard to Find

If progressive education doesn't lend itself to a single fixed definition, that seems fitting in light of its reputation for resisting conformity and standardization. Any two educators who describe themselves as sympathetic to this tradition may well see it differently, or at least disagree about which features are the most important.

Talk to enough progressive educators, in fact, and you'll begin to notice certain paradoxes: Some people focus on the unique needs of individual students, while others invoke the importance of a *community* of learners; some describe learning as a process, more journey than destination, while others believe that tasks should result in authentic products that can be shared.[1]

What It Is

Despite such variations, there are enough elements on which most of us can agree so that a common core of progressive education emerges, however hazily. And it really does make sense to call it a *tradition*, as I did a moment ago. Ironically, what we usually call "traditional" education, in contrast to the progressive approach, has less claim to that adjective—because of how, and how recently, it has developed. As Jim Nehring at the University of Massachusetts at Lowell observed, "Progressive schools are the legacy of a long and proud tradition of thoughtful school practice stretching back for centuries"—including hands-on learning, multiage classrooms, and mentor-apprentice relationships—while what we generally refer to as traditional schooling "is largely the result of outdated policy changes that have calcified into conventions."[2] (Nevertheless, I'll use the conventional nomenclature in this article to avoid confusion.)

It's not all or nothing, to be sure. I don't think I've ever seen a school—even one with scripted instruction, uniforms, and rows of desks bolted to the floor—that has completely escaped the influence of progressive ideas. Nor have I seen a school that's progressive in every detail. Still, schools can be characterized according to how closely they reflect a commitment to values such as these:

Attending to the whole child: Progressive educators are concerned with helping children become not only good learners but also good people. Schooling isn't seen as being about just academics, nor is intellectual growth limited to verbal and mathematical proficiencies.

Community: Learning isn't something that happens to individual children—separate selves at separate desks. Children learn with and from one another in a caring community, and that's true of moral as well as academic learning. Interdependence counts at least as much as independence, so it follows that practices that pit students against one another in some kind of competition, thereby undermining a feeling of community, are deliberately avoided.

Collaboration: Progressive schools are characterized by what I like to call a "working with" rather than a "doing to" model. In place of rewards for complying with the adults' expectations, or punitive consequences for failing to do so, there's more of an emphasis on collaborative problem-solving—and, for that matter, less focus on behaviors than on underlying motives, values, and reasons.

Social justice: A sense of community and responsibility for others isn't confined to the classroom; indeed, students are helped to locate themselves in widening circles of care that extend beyond self, beyond friends, beyond their own ethnic group, and beyond their own country. Opportunities are offered not only to learn about, but also to put into action, a commitment to diversity and to improving the lives of others.

Intrinsic motivation: When considering (or reconsidering) educational policies and practices, the first question that progressive educators are likely to ask is, "What's the effect on students' *interest* in learning, their desire to continue reading, thinking, and questioning?" This deceptively simple test helps to determine what students will and won't be asked to do. Thus, conventional practices, including homework, grades, and tests, prove difficult to justify for anyone who is serious about promoting long-term dispositions rather than just improving short-term skills.

Deep understanding: As the philosopher Alfred North Whitehead declared long ago, "A merely well-informed man is the most useless bore on God's earth." Facts and skills do matter, but only *in a context* and *for a purpose.* That's why progressive education tends to be organized around problems, projects, and questions—rather than around lists of facts, skills, and separate disciplines. The teaching is typically interdisciplinary, the assessment rarely focuses on rote memorization, and excellence isn't confused with "rigor." The point is not merely to challenge students—after all, harder is not necessarily better—but to invite them to think deeply about issues that matter and help them understand ideas from the inside out

Active learning: In progressive schools, students play a vital role in helping to design the curriculum, formulate the questions, seek out (and create) answers, think through possibilities, and evaluate how successful they—and their teachers—have been. Their active participation in every stage of the process is consistent with the overwhelming consensus of experts that learning is a matter of constructing ideas rather than passively absorbing information or practicing skills.

Taking kids seriously: In traditional schooling, as John Dewey once remarked, "the center of gravity is outside the child": he or she is expected to adjust to the school's rules and curriculum. Progressive educators take their cue from the children—and are particularly attentive to differences among them. (Each student is unique, so a single set of policies, expectations, or assignments would be as counterproductive as it was disrespectful.) The curriculum isn't just based on interest, but on *these children's* interests. Naturally, teachers will have broadly conceived themes and objectives in mind, but they don't just design a course of study *for* their students; they design it *with* them, and they welcome unexpected detours. One fourth-grade teacher's curriculum, therefore, won't be the same as that of the teacher next door, nor will her curriculum be the same this year as it was for the children she taught last year. It's not enough to offer elaborate thematic units prefabricated by the adults. And progressive educators realize that the students must help to formulate not only the course of study but also the outcomes or standards that inform those lessons.

Some of the features that I've listed here will seem objectionable, or at least unsettling, to educators at more traditional schools, while others will be surprisingly familiar and may even echo sentiments that they, themselves, have expressed. But progressive educators don't merely *say* they endorse ideas like "love of learning" or "a sense of community." They're willing to put these values into practice even if doing so requires them to up-end traditions. They may eliminate homework altogether if it's clear that students view after-school assignments as something to be gotten over with as soon as possible. They will question things like honors classes and awards assemblies that clearly undermine a sense of community. Progressive schools, in short, follow their core values—bolstered by research and experience—wherever they lead.

What It Isn't

Misconceptions about progressive education generally take two forms. Either it is defined too narrowly so that the significance of the change it represents is understated, or else an exaggerated, caricatured version is presented in order to justify dismissing the whole approach. Let's take each of these in turn.

Individualized attention from caring, respectful teachers is terribly important. But it does not a progressive school make. To assume otherwise not only dilutes progressivism; it's unfair to traditional educators, most of whom are not callous Gradgrinds or ruler-wielding nuns. In fact, it's perfectly consistent to view education as the process of filling children up with bits of knowledge—and to use worksheets, lectures, quizzes, homework, grades, and other such methods in pursuit of that goal—while being genuinely concerned about each child's progress. Schools with warm, responsive teachers who know each student personally can take pride in that fact, but they shouldn't claim on that basis to be progressive.

Moreover, traditional schools aren't always about memorizing dates and definitions; sometimes they're also committed to helping students understand ideas. As one science teacher pointed out, "For thoughtful traditionalists, thinking is couched in terms of comprehending, integrating, and applying knowledge." However, the student's task in such classrooms is "comprehending how the *teacher* has integrated or applied the ideas . . . and [then] reconstruct[ing] the teacher's thinking."[3] There are interesting concepts being discussed in some traditional classrooms, in other words, but what distinguishes progressive education is that students must *construct* their own understanding of ideas.

There's another mistake based on too narrow a definition, which took me a while to catch on to: A school that is culturally progressive is not necessarily educationally progressive. An institution can be steeped in lefty politics and multi-grain values; it can be committed to diversity, peace, and saving the planet—but remain strikingly traditional in its pedagogy. In fact, one can imagine an old-fashioned pour-in-the-facts approach being used to teach lessons in tolerance or even radical politics.[4]

Less innocuous, or accidental, is the tendency to paint progressive education as a touchy-feely, loosey-goosey, fluffy, fuzzy, undemanding exercise in leftover hippie idealism—or Rousseauvian Romanticism. In this cartoon version of the tradition, kids are free to do anything they please, the curriculum can consist of whatever is fun (and nothing that isn't fun). Learning is thought to happen automatically while the teachers just stand by, observing and beaming. I lack the space here to offer examples of this sort of misrepresentation—or a full account of why it's so profoundly wrong—but trust me: People really do sneer at the idea of progressive education based on an image that has little to do with progressive education.

Why It Makes Sense

For most people, the fundamental reason to choose, or offer, a progressive education is a function of their basic values: "a rock-bottom commitment to democracy," as Joseph Featherstone put it; a belief that meeting children's needs should take precedence over preparing future employees; and a desire to nourish curiosity, creativity, compassion, skepticism, and other virtues.

Fortunately, what may have begun with values (for any of us as individuals, and also for education itself, historically speaking) has turned out to be supported by solid data. A truly impressive collection of research has demonstrated that when students are able to spend more time thinking about ideas than memorizing facts and practicing skills—and when they are invited to help direct their own learning—they are not only more likely to enjoy what they're doing but to do it better. Progressive education isn't just more appealing; it's also more productive.

I reviewed decades' worth of research in the late 1990s: studies of preschools and high schools; studies of instruction in reading, writing, math, and science; broad studies of "open classrooms," "student-centered" education, and teaching consistent with constructivist accounts of learning, but also investigations of specific innovations like democratic classrooms, multiage instruction, looping, cooperative learning, and authentic assessment (including the abolition of grades). Across domains, the results overwhelmingly favor progressive education. Regardless of one's values, in other words, this approach can be recommended purely on the basis of its effectiveness. And if your criteria are more ambitious—long-term retention of what's been taught, the capacity to understand ideas and apply them to new kinds of problems, a desire to continue learning—the relative benefits of progressive education are even greater.[5] This conclusion is only strengthened by the *lack* of data to support the value of standardized tests, homework, conventional discipline (based on rewards or consequences), competition, and other traditional practices.[6]

Since I published that research review, similar findings have continued to accumulate. Several newer studies confirm that traditional academic instruction for very young children is counterproductive.[7] Students in elementary and middle school did better in science when their teaching was "centered on projects in which they took a high degree of initiative. Traditional activities, such as completing worksheets and reading primarily from textbooks, seemed to have no positive effect."[8] Another recent study found that an "inquiry-based" approach to learning is more beneficial than conventional methods for low-income and minority students.[9] The results go on and on.[10]

Why It's Rare

Despite the fact that all schools can be located on a continuum stretching between the poles of totally progressive and totally traditional—or, actually, on a series of continuums reflecting the various components of those models—it's usually possible to visit a school and come away with a pretty clear sense of whether it can be classified as predominantly progressive. It's also possible to reach a conclusion about how many schools—or even individual classrooms—in America merit that label: damned few. The higher the grade level, the rarer such teaching tends to be, and it's not even all that prevalent at the lower grades.[11] (Also, while it's probably true that most progressive schools are independent, most independent schools are not progressive.)

The rarity of this approach, while discouraging to some of us, is also rather significant with respect to the larger debate about education. If progressive schooling is actually quite uncommon, then it's hard to blame our problems (real or alleged) on this model. Indeed, the facts have the effect of turning the argument on its head: If students aren't learning effectively, it may be because of the persistence of *traditional* beliefs and practices in our nation's schools.

But we're also left with a question: If progressive education is so terrific, why is it still the exception rather than the rule? I often ask the people who attend my lectures to reflect on this, and the answers that come back are varied and provocative. For starters, they tell me, progressive education is not only less familiar but also much harder to do, and especially to do well. It asks a lot more of the students and at first can seem a burden to those who have figured out how to play the game in traditional classrooms—often succeeding by conventional standards without doing much real thinking. It's also much more demanding of teachers, who have to know their subject matter inside and out if they want their students to "make sense of biology or literature" as opposed to "simply memoriz[ing] the frog's anatomy or the sentence's structure."[12] But progressive teachers also have to know a lot about pedagogy because no amount of content knowledge (say, expertise in science or English) can tell you how to facilitate learning. The belief that anyone who knows enough math can teach it is a corollary of the belief that learning is a process of passive absorption—a view that cognitive science has decisively debunked.

Progressive teachers also have to be comfortable with uncertainty, not only to abandon a predictable march toward the "right answer" but to let students play an active role in the quest for meaning that replaces it. That means a willingness to give up some control and let students take some ownership, which requires guts as well as talent. These characteristics appear not to be as common as we might like to think. Almost a decade ago, I recalled my own experience in high school classrooms with some chagrin: "I prided myself on being an entertaining lecturer, very knowledgeable, funny, charismatic, and so on. It took me years to realize [that my] classroom was all about me, not about the kids. It was about teaching, not about learning."[13] The more we're influenced by the insights of progressive education, the more we're forced to rethink what it means to be a good teacher. That process will unavoidably ruffle some feathers, including our own.

And speaking of feather-ruffling, I'm frequently reminded that progressive education has an uphill journey because of the larger culture we live in. It's an approach that is in some respects inherently subversive, and people in power do not always enjoy being subverted. As Vito Perrone has written, "The values of progressivism—including skepticism, questioning, challenging, openness, and seeking alternate possibilities—have long struggled for acceptance in American society. That they did not come to dominate the schools is not surprising."[14]

There is pressure to raise standardized test scores, something that progressive education manages to do only sometimes and by accident—not only because that isn't its purpose but also because such tests measure what matters least. (The recognition of that fact explains why progressive schools would never dream of using standardized tests as part of their admissions process.) More insidiously, though, we face pressure to standardize our practices in general. Thinking is messy, and deep thinking is really messy. This reality coexists uneasily with demands for order—in schools where the curriculum is supposed to be carefully coordinated across grade levels and planned well ahead of time, or in society at large.

And then (as my audiences invariably point out) there are parents who have never been invited to reconsider their assumptions about education. As a result, they may be impressed by the wrong things, reassured by signs of traditionalism—letter grades, spelling quizzes, heavy textbooks, a teacher in firm control of the classroom—and unnerved by their absence. Even if their children are obviously unhappy, parents may accept that as a fact of life. Instead of wanting the next generation to get better than we got, it's as though their position was: "Listen, if it was bad enough for me, it's bad enough for my kids." If a child is lucky enough to be in a classroom featuring, say, student-designed project-based investigations, the parent may wonder, "But is she really *learning* anything? Where are the worksheets?" And so the teachers feel pressure to make the instruction worse.

All progressive schools experience a constant undertow, perhaps a request to reintroduce grades of some kind, to give special enrichments to the children of the "gifted" parents, to start up a competitive sports program (because American children evidently don't get enough of winning and losing outside of school), to punish the kid who did that bad thing to my kid, to administer a standardized test or two ("just so we can see how they're doing"), and, above all, to get the kids ready for what comes next—even if this amounts to teaching them badly so they'll be prepared for the bad teaching to which they'll be subjected later.[15]

This list doesn't exhaust the reasons that progressive education is uncommon. However, the discussion that preceded it, of progressive education's advantages, was also incomplete, which suggests that working to make it a little more common is a worthy pursuit. We may not be able to transform a whole school, or even a classroom, along all of these dimensions, at least not by the end of this year. But whatever progress we can make is likely to benefit our students. And doing what's best for them is the reason all of us got into this line of work in the first place.

Postscript: A Dozen Questions for Progressive Schools

Because of what I've described as the undertow that progressive educators inevitably experience, it's possible for them to wake up one morning with the unsettling realization that their school has succumbed to a creeping traditionalism and drifted from the vision of its founders. Here are some pointed questions to spur collective reflection and, perhaps, corrective action.

1. Is our school committed to being *educationally* progressive, or is it content with an atmosphere that's progressive only in the political or cultural sense of the word?

2. Is a progressive vision being pursued unapologetically, or does a fear of alienating potential applicants lead to compromising that mission and trying to be all things to all people? ("We offer a nurturing environment . . . of *rigorous* college preparation.")

3. Is the education that the oldest students receive just as progressive as that offered to the youngest, or would a visitor conclude that those in the upper grades seem to attend a different school altogether?

4. Is the teaching organized around problems, projects, and questions? Is most of the instruction truly interdisciplinary, or is literature routinely separated from social studies—or even from spelling? Has acquiring skills (e.g., arithmetic, vocabulary) come to be overemphasized rather than seen as a means to the end of understanding and communicating ideas?

5. To what extent are students involved in designing the curriculum? Is it a learner-centered environment, or are lessons presented to the children as faits accomplis? How much are students involved in other decisions, such as room decoration, classroom manage-

ment, assessment, and so on? Are teachers maintaining control over children, even in subtle ways, so that the classrooms are less democratic than they could be?

6. Is assessment consistent with a progressive vision, or are students evaluated and rated with elaborate rubrics[16] and grade-substitutes? Do students end up, as in many traditional schools, spending so much time thinking about how well they're doing that they're no longer as engaged with *what* they're doing?

7. Do administrators respect teachers' professionalism and need for autonomy—or is there a style of top-down control that's inconsistent with how teachers are urged to treat students? Conversely, is it possible that teachers' insistence on being left alone has permitted them to drift from genuinely progressive practice in some areas?

8. Are educators acting like lifelong learners, always willing to question familiar ways—or do they sometimes fall back on tradition and justify practices on the grounds that something is just "the [name of school] way"? Are teachers encouraged to visit one another's classrooms and offered opportunities to talk about pedagogy on a regular basis?

9. Is cooperation emphasized throughout the school—or are there remnants of an adversarial approach? Do students typically make decisions by trying to reach consensus or do they simply vote? Do competitive games still dominate physical education and even show up in classrooms? Do most learning experiences take place in pairs and small groups, or does the default arrangement consist of having students do things on their own?

10. Is homework assigned only when it's absolutely necessary to extend and enrich a lesson, or is it assigned on a regular basis (as in a traditional school)? If homework is given, are the assignments predicated on—and justified by—a behaviorist model of "reinforcing" what they were taught—or do they truly deepen students' understanding of, and engagement with, ideas? How much of a role do the students play in making decisions about homework?

11. Does the question "How will this affect children's *interest* in learning (and in the topic at hand)?" inform all choices about

curriculum, instruction, and scheduling—or has a focus on right answers and "rigor" led some students to become less curious about, and excited by, what they're doing?

12. Is the school as progressive and collaborative in nonacademic (social, behavioral) matters as it is in the academic realm, or are there remnants of "consequence"-based control such that the focus is sometimes more on order and compliance than on fostering moral reasoning, social skills, and democratic dispositions?

Notes

1. The latter view is represented in both the Reggio Emilia approach to early-childhood education and in the Foxfire tradition.

2. James H. Nehring, "Progressive vs. Traditional: Reframing an Old Debate," *Education Week,* February 1, 2006, p. 32.

3. Mark Windschitl, "Why We Can't Talk to One Another About Science Education Reform," *Phi Delta Kappan,* January 2006, p. 352.

4. As I was preparing this article, a middle-school student of my acquaintance happened to tell me about a class she was taking that featured a scathing indictment of American imperialism—as well as fact-based quizzes and report cards that praised students for being "well behaved" and "on-task."

5. See Alfie Kohn, *The Schools Our Children Deserve: Moving Beyond Traditional Classrooms and "Tougher Standards"* (Boston: Houghton Mifflin, 1999), especially Appendix A.

6. I've tackled each of these issues in separate books. See the sources cited in, respectively, *The Case Against Standardized Testing* (Portsmouth, NH: Heinemann, 2000), *The Homework Myth* (Cambridge, MA: Da Capo Press, 2006), *Beyond Discipline,* rev. ed. (Alexandria, VA: Association for Supervision and Curriculum Development, 2006), and *No Contest: The Case Against Competition,* rev. ed. (Boston: Houghton Mifflin, 1992). Still other research exists to challenge assumptions about the benefits of specific practices ranging from school uniforms to explicit instruction in grammar.

7. See the addendum to "Early-Childhood Education: The Case Against Direct Instruction of Academic Skills" at www.alfiekohn.org/teaching/ece.htm.

8. Harold Wenglinsky, "Facts or Critical Thinking Skills?" *Educational Leadership,* September 2004, p. 33.

9. Michael Klentschy, Leslie Garrison, and Olga Ameral's four-year review

of student achievement data is summarized in Olaf Jorgenson and Rick Vanosdall, "The Death of Science?" *Phi Delta Kappan,* April 2002, p. 604.

10. Also see the comparison of rates of cheating at progressive and traditional schools, mentioned on page 73 of this volume.

11. Educational historian Larry Cuban's review of "almost 7,000 different classroom accounts and results from studies in numerous settings revealed the persistent occurrence of teacher-centered practices since the turn of the century" (*How Teachers Taught: Constancy and Change in American Classrooms, 1890–1980* [New York: Longman, 1984]). John Goodlad, author of the classic study *A Place Called School,* revisited the subject in 1999 and concluded that "although progressive views have enjoyed sufficient visibility to bring down on them and their adherents barrages of negative rhetoric, they have managed to create only isolated islands of practice. . . . Most teachers adhere closely to a view of school as they experienced it as students and so perpetuate the traditional" ("Flow, Eros, and Ethos in Educational Renewal," *Phi Delta Kappan,* April 1999, p. 573). His assessment was corroborated in 2007 by a national study of first, third, and fifth grade classrooms in more than a thousand schools: "Children spent most of their time (91.2%) working in whole-group or individual-seatwork settings" and "the average fifth grader received five times as much instruction in basic skills as instruction focused on problem solving or reasoning; this ratio was 10:1 in first and third grades" (Robert C. Pianta et al., "Opportunities to Learn in America's Elementary Classrooms," *Science* 315 [2007]: 1795). A study of 669 classrooms in Washington State, meanwhile, found that "strong constructivist teaching was observable in about 17 percent of the classroom lessons" (Martin L. Abbott and Jeffrey T. Fouts, "Constructivist Teaching and Student Achievement," Washington School Research Center, Technical Report #5, February 2003, p. 1). For still more evidence, see Kohn, *Schools,* pp. 5–9.

12. David K. Cohen and Carol A. Barnes, "Conclusion: A New Pedagogy for Policy?" in *Teaching for Understanding,* eds. David K. Cohen et al. (San Francisco: Jossey-Bass, 1993), p. 245. The relevance of this point for the largely unsuccessful efforts of progressive education to establish itself over time has been noted by many thinkers, including John Dewey, Lawrence Cremin, and Linda Darling-Hammond.

13. Kitty Thuermer, "In Defense of the Progressive School: An Interview with Alfie Kohn," *Independent School,* Fall 1999, p. 96.

14. Vito Perrone, "Why Do We Need a Pedagogy of Understanding?" in *Teaching for Understanding,* ed. Martha Stone Wiske (San Francisco: Jossey-Bass, 1998), p. 23.

15. For more on this phenomenon, see "Getting Hit on the Head Lessons," which appears as chapter 3 of this volume.

16. See Maja Wilson, *Rethinking Rubrics in Writing Assessment* (Portsmouth, NH: Heinemann, 2006), or my article "The Trouble with Rubrics," which appears as chapter 7 of this volume.

2. Challenging Students— and How to Have More of Them

Learning by doing, a common shorthand for the idea that active participation helps students to understand ideas or acquire skills, is an established principle of progressive education. Much less attention, however, has been paid to the complementary possibility that teachers are most effective when they show rather than just tell. In fact, this idea doesn't even seem to have a name—so let's call it "teaching by doing" (TBD).

Taking Children Backstage

One version of TBD has gained favor in the field of writing instruction,[1] where teachers are urged to reveal their own rough drafts—or, better yet, write things in front of students. It's one thing to analyze the techniques of a story or an essay, a finished product, but it's something else again to observe the process of writing. Particularly if the teacher/writer is narrating, explaining the rationale for choosing this word or that sentence structure, students can witness the false starts, the way errors are made and corrected. In short, they can watch a piece of writing come into being.

There doesn't appear to be much talk about TBD (by any name) in other disciplines; in any case, no one has attempted to connect what may be going on elsewhere with what the writing teachers are doing. But one group of math researchers did comment in passing that "few students get the opportunity to see their teachers engaged in mathematical practice." They went on to cite Berkeley professor Alan Schoenfeld as an impressive exception for inviting his students to bring in problems that he and they could tackle together.[2] Indeed, the wisdom of doing so applies to other fields, too, and shouldn't be limited to graduate seminars. Why, for example, shouldn't students of any age be able to watch their teachers wrestle with meaningful science problems?

It's not unusual, of course, for math teachers to walk students through the steps of solving for x, just as science teachers often do demonstrations to illustrate various laws and principles. But this is teaching by means of scripted performance. It's a matter of going through the motions to show that following certain procedures will produce predictable results. Students are then instructed to imitate what they've seen.

What intrigues me, by contrast, is having a science teacher actually conduct a public experiment, one that students may have helped to design and one whose outcome is uncertain. In such classrooms, teachers can be heard to say things like: "I'm not sure what's going to happen here, but let's take a stab at it." Those who teach science by doing science spend a lot of time erasing or crossing out, as do their colleagues who teach writing by writing.

That there are similarities between what's done in language arts and in science or mathematics isn't so surprising. But it occurs to me that one might also draw a parallel between teaching any academic subject and teaching morality. It's widely accepted that, in order for children to learn to be good people, they should be *shown* how to act. Parents in particular try to set an example by the way they treat others. And, indeed, some studies suggest that children are more likely to donate to charity if they've watched someone else do so. On the other hand, modeling doesn't always work on its own. In fact, there is evidence that "exposure to paragons of helpfulness may undermine the intrinsic motivation to help."[3] Young adults who watched highly helpful people came to view themselves as less altruistic.

Part of the problem is that modeling is a concept rooted in behaviorism. It began as a refinement of the principles of operant and classical conditioning. Those principles couldn't account for the fact that people sometimes learn from what they've observed, acting in ways for which they themselves received no reinforcement. But modeling, like reinforcing, is just another technique for getting someone to behave in a particular way; it doesn't necessarily promote a dedication to, or an understanding of, that behavior. Because mere imitation doesn't achieve those more ambitious goals, we need to supplement the showing with telling—the precise inverse of what I've proposed for academic instruction in classrooms.

It may make sense not only to use explanation as a separate strategy alongside modeling, but to combine the two approaches into what might be called "deep modeling." Here, we not only set an example for children but try to make it clear to them what we're doing and why we're doing it. Verbalizing is a familiar strategy to many of us, from self-talk therapies to the technique known as "think aloud" that's intended to help students comprehend more of what they read. Deep modeling is different in that the narration is coming from someone else.

Consider the challenge of real-world ethical conundrums. It's fine for parents to try to model honesty and compassion for their children, but what happens when those two values seem to pull in opposite directions—for example, when telling the truth may hurt someone's feelings? Similarly, it's easy to say that kids should look out for other people's interests, but to what extent must they give up something they enjoy so that someone else will benefit?

We can let children know how *we* think (and feel) our way through similar dilemmas by describing to them the factors that we consider in making such decisions: the relevance of our previous experiences, the principles from which we're operating, and all the thoughts and emotions that we take into account. From watching and listening to us, kids not only learn more about how we try to live a moral life; they also figure out that morality is rarely cut-and-dried.

Deep modeling might be thought of as a way of taking children "backstage." To that extent, it's very much like writing—or conducting an authentic science experiment—in front of them. They're able to experience what happens before (or behind or beneath) the ethical decisions that adults make, the essays they publish, and the scientific principles they discover—all of which are usually presented to children as completed products.

This has several advantages, the most obvious of which is that experiencing the process helps them to become more proficient. The main reason language arts specialists think students should have the chance to watch their teachers write is so these students will learn more about, and get better at, the craft of writing. By the same token, children presumably would become more skillful at solving math problems, or make better moral decisions, as a result of seeing how adults do those things.

Another benefit of demonstration is the possibility that students will be more likely to *want* to do what they've seen. As a rule, educational researchers and theorists are much less focused on disposition than on achievement. For every article that looks at motivational issues—students' attitudes and goals and interests—there are scores dealing exclusively with skills and outcomes. That fact helps to explain the popularity of forms of teaching and assessment that cause students to think of learning as a chore—which, paradoxically, can have devastating results on achievement over the long haul. More attention to how students feel about what they're doing could lead to innumerable improvements in instruction and curriculum. One such strategy is teaching by doing. All else being equal, a student is more likely to become intrigued about something that he or she actually sees someone do.

De-mist-ification
Enhancing skills and disposition are impressive accomplishments, to be sure, but there's something else to be gained by taking children backstage that frankly interests me even more. The third benefit is rarely discussed, possibly because it's inherently more controversial: Teaching by doing can change how children regard the activity in question, the people who engage in the activity, and the very idea of authority. It has, in a word, a powerful debunking function.

When I was a teacher, I always made a point of stopping any student who used the plural pronoun when talking about a book: "They say on page 87 that . . ." What bothered me was not the grammatical error (assuming only one person wrote the book), but the disappearance of the author into the indefinite "they." Authors are fallible and have distinctive points of view, I reminded my classes. When we lose sight of the person behind the words, we forget that those words can be challenged.

Exactly the same thing happens when students encounter a series of finished products, whether they are books, scientific laws, or ethical precepts. Thus, one solution is to allow them to watch something being written, or proved, or decided, in order to make the activity in question more accessible and less intimidating. Good writing or thinking isn't up there and out of reach, done only by others and handed down to us. Rather, it's something students realize they might be able to do themselves, even if they can't do it all that well yet.

Equally important, the solutions, conclusions, compositions, and decisions that are set out as examples are not immune from the students' critical inspection. And by demystifying the activity, we demystify the people engaged in the activity. Or perhaps I should say "de*mist*ify," given that we're helping students to dissipate the fog of authority that surrounds teachers, parents, and other adults. This is only likely to happen, however, if we're willing to make it clear that we—not just those other grown-ups out there—are fallible. That's why I say that staged, scripted demonstrations won't do; kids have to see us chugging down blind alleys and shifting into reverse. John Holt lamented that we adults so often "present ourselves to children as if we were gods, all-knowing, all-powerful, always rational, always just, always right. This is worse than any lie we could tell about ourselves." In order to counteract this tendency, he continued, "When I am trying to do something I am no good at . . . I do it in front of [students] so they can see me struggling with it."4

What makes teaching by doing so valuable to students is precisely what leads so many adults to resist it. There's something reassuring to most of us about playing the role of the crisply competent, always authoritative Teacher-with-a-capital-T, and we're loath to relinquish it. If we take kids backstage, if we publicly work on a problem we may not be able to solve, we feel vulnerable. We fear that we may lose some control.

In fact, students, too, may resist authentic teaching—at least at first. For one thing, they may prefer to avoid unnecessary intellectual challenges such as those entailed by a more active, probing form of learning. The introduction of a nontraditional science program led one tenth grader to exclaim, "We see what all this is about now.

You are trying to get us to think and learn for ourselves." Exactly right, replied the teacher, relieved and grateful that the message was getting through. "Well," the student continued, "we don't want to do that."[5]

It's not just about how much effort is required. Students may become accustomed to classrooms in which they aren't expected (or even permitted) to have much of a say about what happens.[6] And they may grow comfortable with the idea that books are sacred texts, or with the reduction of scientific discovery to the following of recipes, or with the premise that each ethical problem has a single right answer waiting to be uncovered, or even with a vision of adults as dispensers of unquestionable wisdom.[7]

It takes considerable effort, not to mention courage, to call these preferences and assumptions into question and to persuade students of the value of becoming truly critical thinkers. After all, from their first days in school they have been carefully instructed in what Philip Jackson famously called the "hidden curriculum": how to do what you're told and stay out of trouble. There are rewards, both tangible and symbolic, for those who behave properly and penalties for those who don't. Students are trained to sit still, copy down what the teacher says, and run their highlighters across whatever words in the book they expect to be asked to memorize. Pretty soon, they become less likely to ask (or even wonder), "Does that really make sense?"—and more likely to ask, "Is this going to be on the test?"

As a brand-new high school teacher some years ago, I resolved to let my students know that this passivity was not what I was looking for. On my very first day, I proudly—and, given the culture of the school, somewhat defiantly—pinned a yellow button to my shirt that said QUESTION AUTHORITY. Alas, this concept was so unfamiliar to the students that some of them assumed the phrase was a descriptive label rather than an exhortation. One girl wanted to know who had appointed me the school's question authority.

This is essentially the same state of affairs that Norm Diamond, an Oregon educator and labor activist, was trying to capture when he invented a syndrome called Compliance Acquiescent Disorder (CAD). He intended it as a spoof of Oppositional Defiant Disorder (ODD), for which countless children are referred for treatment. A local newspaper ran an advertisement that itemized the symptoms of ODD ("argues with adults," "actively defies rules") and invited parents who thought they had such children to allow them to be given an experimental medication. In response, Diamond placed a counter-ad about CAD in the paper. An individual with this disorder, it explained, "defers to authority," "actively obeys rules," "fails to argue back," "knuckles under instead of mobilizing others in support," "stays restrained when outrage is warranted," and so on.[8] If excessive compliance and acquiescence really were defined as a disorder, there's no telling how many millions of children would have to be treated for it. In reality, though, not only do few people regard it as a problem, but it seems to be the very point of the training the students receive.

Passivity, however, is not the only outcome of that training. We may also witness a diminution of interest in the life of the mind. Even those who are successful at playing the game of school and managing to stifle the urge to ask impertinent questions may find what they've been doing deeply unappealing on some level. If they haven't been exposed to a more active, more critical model of learning, they may well walk away from all intellectual pursuits. Another possible consequence of enforced passivity is, paradoxically, a belated revolt. Adults can get away with presenting themselves as absolute authorities for a while, but children eventually come to realize how flawed and fallible their mentors really were—or, rather, are. What follows is a painful process of disillusion, a resentful awareness of having been misled, and sometimes an exaggerated, angry, and unconstructive form of rebellion. This may happen during adolescence or much later. Even if it never happens, though, it's difficult to overstate how much damage has been done, how many opportunities have been lost, as a result of an education designed mostly to create acceptance.

Needed: Questioners and Challengers

The idea that we ought to help children become more challenging, more willing to stand up to authority, will seem both curious and objectionable to adults who view kids as too rude, loud, and rebellious already. The central mission of many books (and workshops) on the subject of classroom management is to create a more efficient environment for the teacher to pursue her agenda, and that generally entails heading off inconvenient challenges from students. Of course, this tells us more about the desire for compliance on the part of the people who write and read these books than it does about what children are like.

Part of the disagreement between those who want to see students challenge what they're told and those who think students are entirely too challenging as it is may be due not to incompatible values but to the ambiguity of words like *challenging*. I don't deny that some students are rude and aggressive, and I don't want more of them to be that way. This is not a brief for obnoxiousness or for mindless, if-you-say-yes-then-I'll-say-no opposition. Rather, I'm arguing for the value of reasoned objections and principled skepticism. Thus, it's possible to assert, without contradicting oneself, that some students are unpleasant and also that too many students are unwilling to challenge authority.

The fact that childhood is an ideal time to begin promoting the disposition to question and speak out doesn't mean that only children are unlikely to do these things at present. Quite the opposite. All around us we find adults who sound like Robert Frost's neighbor, the man who "will not go beyond his father's saying." All around us are people who, when questioned about some habit or belief they have adopted, reply, "Well, that's just the way I was raised"—as if this ended the conversation, as if it were impossible to critically examine the values with which one was raised.

All around us we encounter individuals who not only are unwilling to oppose that which is wrong, but who seem not even to *see* that something is wrong. They open their front door, survey a landscape of suffering and injustice, and quietly close the door again, declaring with satisfaction that all is well. All around us—including in the field of education—we meet people who have lost their capacity to be outraged by outrageous things, people who, when they are handed foolish and destructive mandates, respond by meekly asking for guidance on how to put them into practice. If they ever had the gumption to analyze ("Is this really in children's best interest?") or to object (when the answer to that question is no), it has long since evaporated.

Even if our only goal were to understand the world more accurately, we would need to maintain a questioning stance. Intellectual progress demands that we refuse to take things at face value, refuse to accept everything we've been told, refuse to assume that the conventional wisdom must be right. Science, as Richard Feynman remarked, can be defined as "the belief in the ignorance of authority"[9]—a statement that might be dismissed as hyperbolic were it not for Feynman's eminence as a scientist.

Of course, that same questioning stance is demanded not only by a desire to understand but by a desire to act, not only to find out what is true but to do what is right. There are social and political realities that fail to meet even the most elementary standard of moral acceptability. Rather than socializing children to accept things the way they are—accept them as desirable or, just as bad, accept them as inevitable—we need to help children critically analyze the status quo in order to decide which institutions and traditions are worth keeping and which need to be changed. In short, we should help students "talk back to the world."[10]

Some who would like to see students do just that are inclined to turn, logically enough, to the movement known as Critical Thinking (CT), which was all the rage among educators during the 1980s.[11] Alas, CT proves disappointingly traditional in several respects:

• To respond to ideas and events critically, one must not only think but also feel, care, and do. CT, as the name implies, is an exclusively cognitive affair.

• A CT curriculum trains students to master a set of discrete analytical skills; they learn to spot this logical fallacy, then that one. Here we find the familiar behaviorist tendency to reduce a whole to its parts.

• Each of those skills is transmitted from teacher to student, which leaves the relationship between them unexamined. CT is about analyzing arguments, not about questioning the role of authority.

• Like most instruction, CT is geared to improving the proficiency of individual students. Meaningful criticism, on the other hand, is a social process—not merely logical but dialogical—and it addresses the structural causes of the situations in which we find ourselves.

• Finally, and implicit in the preceding points, CT is concerned only with what students are able to do, not with whether they're inclined to do it. They may learn what "*post hoc, ergo propter hoc*" means, and they may be able to recognize the use of loaded language when they see it. But will they use these tools? And, if so, when and to what end? CT is so far removed from promoting a critical sensibility that one begins to suspect the word "critical" in its name is intended in the other sense, as a synonym for "important." Done well, CT can indeed help students to acquire useful thinking skills, but it's not about helping them to *become* critical, to talk back to the world.[12] For that, we need other measures. One such measure is the practice of taking children backstage. But there is much more that educators can do.

Raising Rebels

From about age five, children tend to latch onto the concept of fairness, denouncing whatever they believe violates that ideal. Teachers can build on this principle, extending it beyond self-interest so that students realize it's unacceptable when any person (or group) has been wronged. At the same time, it makes sense to call attention to wrongs that are, in fact, taking place and support the process of developing and refining a sense of moral outrage. The goal is to help children acquire the insight needed to recognize injustices and the courage needed to oppose them. Here, of course, we are trafficking in values, but in a way quite different from—perhaps even diametrically opposed to—the orientation of mainstream "character education," which is usually more about socializing children to accept status-quo values than to challenge them.[13]

It's possible, however, to promote a critical sensibility even without discrete lessons devoted to social and ethical issues. What matters most is how the regular curriculum is taught. In many cases, teachers may come to realize that the default approach to instruction has the effect of inculcating passivity, with students spending most of their time swallowing right answers and then spitting them back on command. This process is easy to see where scripted instruction is used—or, even more commonly, in classrooms characterized by the unholy trinity of textbooks, tests, and lectures.

But I've been struck by how many teachers who regard themselves as nontraditional, or as champions of critical thinking, also end up promoting passivity in ways they probably don't intend. I recently visited a combined third- and fourth-grade classroom at a nominally progressive school and watched as the two teachers met separately with students for a math lesson. In both groups, the agenda consisted mostly of reviewing the students' answers to worksheet questions about place value. One boy rattled off an elaborate technique he had devised for solving a problem, after which the teacher, in a rather perfunctory fashion, said, "Wow. I'd have to look at that." It was clear from his tone, and from the fact that he quickly moved on to the next problem, that he had no plans of investigating the idea any further. The boy and his classmates presumably got the message that innovative thinking was not encouraged here. Across the room, meanwhile, the other teacher was trying to help her students figure out what "they"—the anonymous worksheet creators—meant by a certain instruction. The goal was to second-guess the intentions of distant authorities and then do what they wanted.[14]

There is a striking difference between a lesson—and, over time, a classroom—whose purpose is to train students to provide correct responses and one whose purpose is to promote deep understanding. Even in math, where right answers obviously exist, some teachers deliberately avoid presenting (or at least minimize the salience of) the accepted algorithm. Instead, they invite students to invent their own techniques and to discuss with one another why each may have gotten a different answer. Even when a student comes up with the correct answer, such teachers are apt to ask, "How else could you figure it out?"

The more traditional approach, by contrast, is to scan children's ideas to determine the extent of their "correspondence [with] what the teacher wanted," as Eleanor Duckworth saw it. "Knowing the right answer requires no decisions, carries no risks, and makes no demands. It is automatic. It is thoughtless." The single-minded concern with getting children to produce that answer, Duckworth added, may offer one response to the haunting question: "What happens to children's curiosity and resourcefulness later in their childhood?"[15] However, curiosity and resourcefulness are not the only casualties of this kind of teaching; students' inclination to object, to resist, to refuse to be cowed by authority is also affected. We should reject a focus on right answers and conventional methods, in other words, not only because it promotes shallow learning but because it promotes passive acceptance.

Avoiding practices that encourage passivity is just the beginning, of course. Teachers also must take steps to create critical classrooms and to set up regular opportunities for students to be skeptical about what they hear. The choice of reading matter plays a role here. When a teacher deliberately assigns material that contains errors or clear indications of the author's point of view, students can be jolted into the recognition that something in print shouldn't be accepted at face value. The teacher can help students develop the disposition and the skills necessary to notice mistakes and biases even in works where these things may not be so close to the surface.

Some elements of this process require exquisite skill on the teacher's part, but others are quite straightforward. They can be as simple as explicitly inviting students to ask probing questions—and modeling such questions for them, if necessary. These opportunities should be built into the curriculum so that every lesson includes chances to wonder, to argue, to criticize the text and what the teacher has said. At least initially, it may be wise to have students engage in this process in small groups, which, as Ira Shor points out, allows them "to gain confidence and to develop a position collectively . . . so there is less chance of students being silenced by the teacher's . . . comments on the issue."[16]

The content of one's teaching makes as much of a difference as the style. The subject matter of particular disciplines can be framed so as to highlight examples of dissent, with students learning about people who have challenged established ways of painting or governing or thinking about the natural world. To take a rather different example, instead of just defining the word *metaphor* and assigning students to locate examples in a work of literature, metaphors can be introduced as a kind of rebellion against things as they are. There is something implicitly subversive about the project of imposing different and deeper meanings on the world we encounter.

Or consider the social scientist Herbert Simon's distinction between "well-structured" problems, the kind that are clearly defined and can be solved by applying established algorithms, and "ill-structured" problems, which are complex and don't necessarily contain all the information necessary for solving them or even clear criteria for determining whether they've been solved. The latter are much more realistic given that "all the really important social, political, and scientific problems in the world today . . . are ill-structured,"[17] and they're also more likely to provoke students to question what they're told.

Here's another specific suggestion for promoting a critical perspective: Teachers can emphasize the ideas in a given field that they are still personally struggling to make sense of. The passion they probably feel about such issues is likely to facilitate students' engagement even as it communicates two equally important messages: that people continue to be genuinely curious all their lives and that adults, including teachers, may be uncertain and even clueless about some things. The latter point can also be made by focusing a discussion on what even the experts still don't understand—that is, on what *isn't* known—in a given field. Or teachers might present "a major disciplinary issue about which experts of equal stature disagree dramatically," after which students can be asked "how it is possible for experts to come to such different conclusions"[18]—and for so many absolute certainties about the world to have been questioned and ultimately overturned.

Even while reviewing basic facts and skills, teachers can emphasize that many things we just accept as givens could have been otherwise. It's helpful to know how many ounces are in a pound, but it's much more important to understand the lack of any transcendent rationale for dividing up a pound that way or for using pounds as a unit of weight in the first place. So, too, should children be reminded how arbitrary the "correct"—which is only to say, conventional— spellings of words really are. Toward that end, teachers might present sentences featuring words that have more than one acceptable spelling or whose spelling has changed over time. ("My *loveable advisor cancelled* our meeting about the *esthetic* features of the new *catalog*.") One can take an active and critical stance, in other words, even toward basic knowledge that students need to acquire.

Thoughtful assignments can be designed specifically to encourage a sharper, more active response to authors. It's possible to dispense with the tired practice of asking students whether they agree or disagree with what they've read. "*Why* do you agree or disagree?" is a little better, insofar as it invites reflection, but even that question is far from ideal. To begin with, it suggests that there are only two possible responses. (Exercises in which students are assigned to argue for or against a given proposition, like anthologies that contain clashing "pro" and "con" articles on controversial issues, similarly teach students to think in simplistic and misleading dualities.) We want students to construct nuanced positions on important questions, not merely to come out for or against something.[19]

Asking students for their opinion about what they've read, rather than whether they agree or disagree with it, would seem to address this concern. But even here we have to be careful. The premise of both questions seems to be that the student's view is a fixed reference point by which ideas should be evaluated. This excludes the possibility that one's opinion might change as a result of having been exposed to a new idea. Thus asking "What questions do you have that you didn't have before you read this?" is more consistent with the possibility that *learning* might have taken place.

The implication here is that, while students are questioning what they read and challenging what they're taught, they should also be questioning and challenging their own beliefs. This is Constructivism 101: Learning happens when we're compelled to reorganize our thinking in light of a fresh experience or when we discover that two beliefs can't easily be reconciled. It's not always recognized, though, that an approach intended to promote a more sophisticated mastery of ideas can also promote the disposition to challenge. Moreover, it should be emphasized that such a disposition applies to others and oneself alike. To be critical only of other people's ideas is to risk arrogance and stagnation; to be critical only of one's own ideas is to risk timidity and indecision.

It takes time, of course, to help students learn to strike the right balance or, for that matter, to do almost any of the things I've been talking about. Deep inquiry and critical evaluation are much less likely to take place if the curriculum has been overplanned or if learning must conform to a rigid schedule. The worst-case scenario is the concatenation of short periods in a factory-like high school, but many elementary teachers voluntarily impose something almost as bad, cutting off discussion about the presidential election because an arbitrary timetable inscribed on the blackboard dictates that "it's time now to take out our science books."

One common theme in all these suggestions is the happy confluence between the kind of teaching that helps students learn better and the kind that helps them challenge the world as they find it. This is true not only of the specific topics and methods I've been discussing, but also of certain overarching educational goals that have been proposed for stimulating intellectual development. Consider the five "habits of mind" developed by Deborah Meier and her colleagues. The study of virtually any topic will benefit, they argue, from raising questions about *evidence* ("How do we know what we know?"), *point of view* ("Whose perspective does this represent?"), *connections* ("How is this related to that?"), *supposition* ("How might things have been otherwise?"), and *relevance* ("Why is this important?").[20] When you think about it, these are also habits of "minding"—that is, of objecting and shaking one's head and speaking out. Educators who navigate by the questions Meier proposes—as opposed to, say, by the criterion of standardized test scores—are likely to help students become skeptical and perhaps even brave.

Why, then, are so many students compelled to spend so much

time practicing skills and memorizing right answers? Perhaps it's because those with an interest in preserving the status quo don't want kids (or even most adults) to feel too confident or empowered. It isn't surprising, Paulo Freire remarked, that "the 'banking' concept of education," in which knowledge is deposited in student receptacles, regards people as "adaptable, manageable beings. The more students work at storing the deposits entrusted to them"—a pretty good summary of most homework—"the less they develop [a] critical consciousness."[21] There may be good reason, in other words, for conservatives to oppose constructivism, learner-centered instruction, whole language, and the like; conversely, there may be good reason for socially and politically progressive people to be over-represented among the proponents of such teaching.[22]

Many philosophers and politicians believe that education is principally about transmitting a set of cultural beliefs to children in order to reproduce our institutions and values in the next generation. Conservatives, almost by definition, are likely to take this position, but in the United States, the range of debate on many issues has been narrowed to the point that mainstream thinkers, the only kind given a respectful hearing, tend to agree about far more than they disagree. Basic premises are accepted across the visible political spectrum. Thus, for example, William Galston, a political theorist who advised President Clinton and other Democrats, has declared that the state may not "prescribe curricula or pedagogic practices that require or strongly invite students to become skeptical or critical of their own way of life." After quoting that remarkable statement, Nel Noddings adds, "Socrates would weep. But, of course, people who feared critical thinking in his time knew what to do with Socrates."[23]

Climate and Culture

To challenge is to venture out on uncertain terrain, and in order to take such risks, one must first experience a sense of safety. Students have to feel comfortable if they're going to promote useful discomfort for themselves and those around them. This applies not only to high-profile dissent but to high-quality thought. One educator, defending the need to explore "the affective aspects of cognition," emphasized that "to engage in thinking which is challenging, fraught with ambiguity, and involves reflective activity necessarily requires students to feel confident in their ability to make sense of problematic situations."[24] This is doubly true if students are engaged in *making* situations problematic.

While temperamental differences will incline some people to feel more confident and comfortable than others, teachers can work with all students to create a caring classroom community, a place where everyone feels valued and supported and no one fears being laughed at for asking a question or proposing an idea.

Creating a classroom that's conducive to challenge is a matter of what teachers do, but also of what they refrain from doing. It's a function of their personalities (warm and inviting versus chilly and intimidating), but also of the way teaching and learning are structured. I'm not interested only in whether a teacher smiles and nods and hugs, but in whether he or she schedules class meetings devoted explicitly to eliminating putdowns and helping reticent students to feel comfortable about speaking up. I'm also interested in whether students are publicly evaluated, whether their assignments are graded, whether they have been led to focus more on *how well* they're doing in school than on *what* they're doing. Even in the classrooms of supportive teachers ("Ooh, you're close!" or "I'm sure you'll do better next time!"), learning often takes a back seat to performance. And many students will decline to challenge the person who serves as the arbiter of their performance. "In order not to fail," the anthropologist Jules Henry once observed, "most students are willing to believe anything and [not to care] whether what they are told is true or false."[25] The hidden curriculum in such classrooms is how to please authority, not how to develop convictions and stand up for them.

It's important to add that a classroom can be safe and supportive while promoting criticism and even rebellion. Some years ago, David and Roger Johnson, the cooperative-learning mavens, and some of their students (including Dean Tjosvold, now a management theorist), formulated the idea of "cooperative conflict" or "constructive controversies."[26] Its premise is that we don't need to choose between an environment that's adversarial, in which one person's success is predicated on another's failure, and one in which disagreement is discouraged. Neither is desirable. A setting with contests, debates, and an imperative to triumph over others feels chronically unsafe, as I've argued elsewhere. But a setting characterized by enforced harmony isn't exactly an incubator of courage or effective problem solving. That's why Alfred Sloan, who ran General Motors in the 1920s, was known for saying to his board of directors, "I take it we're all in complete agreement on this decision? In that case, let's postpone further discussion of the matter until our next meeting to give ourselves time to develop disagreement and perhaps gain some understanding of what the decision is all about."

Cooperative conflict offers the best of both worlds: the passion of disagreement nested in a caring community. Lessons can be structured with this blend in mind, and its very existence in the classroom serves to remind students of the possibility of civil discord, or noncompetitive argument, or what the Johnson brothers once called "friendly excursions into disequilibrium."

Ideally, teachers are open not only to having students challenge one another, but also to having students challenge *them*. This is the logical conclusion of the idea of taking students backstage and demystifying one's authority, which I described earlier. However, it's a conclusion that many teachers find difficult to reach. Don't get me wrong. I'm convinced they'd like children to think for themselves, to be assertive and morally courageous . . . with their friends. All teachers hope students will resist peer pressure, but they may be "troubled by children's passivity only in certain contexts," as psychologist Robert Deluty pointed out. They don't want kids to be bullied, but they want them to follow directions from adults uncritically.[27]

We have to be secure enough to welcome challenges without becoming defensive or reverting to practices that are fundamentally autocratic. We need to remind ourselves just how much social, moral, and intellectual growth will be sacrificed when getting or keeping control of the classroom is our paramount goal. (Countless discipline manuals offer advice for how best to outmaneuver children who have the temerity to argue with us, how best to parry—or, better yet, preempt—their challenges. Such books provide excellent examples of what not to do and how not to be.[28])

No specific expertise is required to take this advice. An openness to being confronted by one's students is more a matter of will than skill. But two theorists have suggested interesting ways of taking the basic idea a step further. Frank Smith recommends bringing a second adult into the classroom, someone able and willing to argue with the teacher. This empowers students to do the same—or at least to avoid thinking of the teacher as an absolute authority figure whose ideas must be accepted.[29]

Meanwhile, Marilyn Watson, an expert on early childhood development, proposes that we not only make it clear to children that their opinions count (by listening carefully and giving their views a respectful hearing), but that we also refrain from "responding with the full force of our argument to justify our own positions, thereby overwhelming children with our logic." In fact, she adds, we should "help children develop reasons to support their own views, even if we don't agree with those views. We should help them to articulate their position, or even marshal the best argument [we] can think of from their perspective." The ultimate goal, after all, isn't to ensure that our position prevails, but to encourage children to challenge us (and others) and to help them learn how to frame their arguments more convincingly. We want kids to talk back to us, as long as they do so respectfully, and we want them to get better at it.[30]

To suggest that teachers relinquish the comfortable position of authority over students is to ask a lot, especially if most of *their* teachers, from preschool to graduate school, haven't set a particularly daring example. For that matter, any change that entails rethinking basic questions about the teacher/student relationship and the objectives of schooling is more likely to take hold if, as a matter of policy, teachers are treated as professionals and trusted to use their judgment. They need to feel safe about taking risks in order to create classrooms where students can feel the same way; it's hard to give others what you, yourself, don't have. A teacher who has been deluged with directives and intimidated into following orders is rarely able to help students find the courage to dissent.

Schools of education have a fundamental choice to make here.[31] Teacher educators can either socialize their students to deal with educational reality as they find it and try to succeed within given conditions, or they can encourage their students to ask radical (that is, root) questions. Those who see the latter as their mission will provide future teachers not only with what they'll need to do their job well but also with what they'll need to re-imagine and reshape the job that's been defined for them. Newly minted educators may benefit from a familiarity with different theories of education, but they also need what Hemingway called a good crap detector. They ought to emerge from the university secure in the belief that one can and must fight what is wrong, rather than being inclined to put their heads down and hope it will go away by itself.

It may be necessary for some teacher educators to take a hard look at what happens in their own classrooms. It's not uncommon to find university instructors who see themselves as critical thinkers, progressive and even radical critics of the status quo, but who rely on orthodox pedagogical methods to transmit heterodox ideas. Some of their courses are done *to*, rather than designed *with*, students; the syllabuses are written before the course has even begun. Some of these instructors proceed largely by lecturing, by fishing for right answers during discussions, even by giving grades. And that is the chief lesson their students will take away: not the explicit content of the course, but the idea that classrooms are places where students listen and memorize facts and figure out how to snag a good mark. Ideally, professors of education should not only reconsider their own reliance on the usual practices but should attempt to do in their classrooms the kinds of things I've been describing, beginning with taking their students backstage in order to demystify the process of teaching (including teaching about teaching).

Regardless of what or whom one teaches, there are ways to help students develop an active and critical stance. Obviously the strategies listed here are not exhaustive. In fact, I would be grateful to hear from educators about their experiences with any approach that has proved useful for reaching the same objectives.[32] We need to learn from—and, fittingly, to challenge—one another's ideas. But most important is a basic commitment to make sure that our students— future teachers, parents, and citizens—are able and willing to take a stand.

Notes

1. For example, see the work of Donald Graves, Nancie Atwell, Regie Rout-man, and Donald Murray.

2. John Seely Brown, Allan Collins, and Paul Duguid, "Situated Cognition and the Culture of Learning," *Educational Researcher,* January/February 1989, pp. 32–42. Schoenfeld himself has argued that students not only don't get to see their instructor doing problems but don't really get to do problems themselves. "Over the period of a full school year, none of the students in any of the dozen classes we observed [in a highly regarded suburban high school] worked mathematical tasks that could seriously be called prob-lems. What the students worked were exercises: tasks designed to indicate mastery of relatively small chunks of subject matter, and to be completed in a short amount of time." The focus was not on "mathematical think-ing" but on "the rote memorization of facts and procedures" (Alan H. Schoenfeld, "When Good Teaching Leads to Bad Results: The Disasters of 'Well-Taught' Mathematics Courses," *Educational Psychologist* 23 [1988]: 159, 164).

3. I reviewed several studies on modeling and generosity in *The Brighter Side of Human Nature* (New York: Basic Books, 1990). The cautionary study is George C. Thomas, C. Daniel Batson, and Jay S. Coke, "Do Good Samari-tans Discourage Helpfulness?" *Journal of Personality and Social Psychology* 40 (1981): 194–200.

4. John Holt, *How Children Fail,* rev. ed. (New York: Delta, 1982), pp. 282–83. This, I suspect, is similar to the reason the Mission Hill School in Boston, founded by Deborah Meier, has its main office in the same large room where students use computers or just hang out. There are no secrets when staff members meet or talk on the phone. For the most part, the inner workings of school administration are deliberately transparent to everyone.

5. This exchange was reported in Richard T. White, "Raising the Quality of Learning: Principles from Long-Term Action Research," in *Effective and*

Responsible Teaching: The New Synthesis, eds. Fritz K. Oser et al. (San Francisco: Jossey-Bass, 1992), p. 55.

6. After years of being instructed to comply with someone else's decisions, it can be disconcerting to be invited to do some of the deciding. This is a point I raised more than a decade ago, at the end of an article that emphasized the importance of giving students more say about what happens in their classrooms. I suggested that resistance on the part of students takes three primary forms: *refusing* to participate in making choices ("You're the teacher—that's your job!"); *testing* (that is, offering outrageous suggestions or responses to see if the teacher is serious about sharing authority); and *parroting* (repeating stock teacher lines or guessing what the teacher wants to hear). See "Choices for Children," *Phi Delta Kappan,* September 1993, pp. 8–20, available at www.alfiekohn.org/teaching/cfc.htm.

7. Moreover, even those students who welcome the chance to challenge received wisdom and to see teachers as fellow learners may need to be convinced that an adult is what he or she claims to be. As Carl Rogers once remarked, "Students have been 'conned' for so long that a teacher who is real with them is usually seen for a time as simply exhibiting a new brand of phoniness"; see *A Way of Being* (Boston: Houghton Mifflin, 1980), p. 273.

8. Norm Diamond, "Defiance Is Not a Disease," *Rethinking Schools,* Summer 2003, p. 13.

9. Feynman's comment, published in his book *The Pleasure of Finding Things Out,* was cited in an article by David Berliner that was, in turn, cited by Gerald Bracey in his April 2004 *Phi Delta Kappan* column.

10. The idea of "talking back" to authority is credited to the writer bell hooks by the editors of *Rethinking Schools,* who used the phrase in their 2003 book *Rethinking School Reform.* This sensibility is sometimes articulated by academic theorists whose critiques of conventional education require one to hack through a dense tangle of off-putting, self-important verbiage: "liberatory praxis," "problematizing discourse," "textual hegemonies," "conflictual domains of materiality," and so on. There are useful ideas lurking in many such monographs, to be sure, but after reading them, one is sometimes left with the impression that a few hundred academics and graduate students are talking to one another and using lots of words (many of them nearly inaccessible) where a few would do. Meanwhile, ten-year-olds are still being trained to think the teacher knows everything, the textbook is always right, only kids screw up, and education is about memorizing the right answer.

11. It was all the rage, that is, until it was supplanted by Total Quality Management, then by Outcome-Based Education, then by Brain-Based Education,

and then by Differentiated Instruction. There may have been a few more in there, too.

12. Some of these criticisms of CT, along with several others, are raised by the contributors to *Perspectives in Critical Thinking: Essays by Teachers in Theory and Practice,* Danny Weil and Holly Kathleen Anderson, eds. (New York: Peter Lang, 2000).

13. See my essay "How Not to Teach Values: A Critical Look at Character Education," *Phi Delta Kappan,* February 1997, pp. 429–39, available at www.alfiekohn.org/teaching/hnttv.htm. It, along with "Choices for Children" (cited previously), was reprinted in *What to Look for in a Classroom . . . and Other Essays* (San Francisco: Jossey-Bass, 1998).

14. "Teachers who have a limited view of mathematical knowledge . . . [treat] the mathematics textbook . . . as a cryptic but authoritative document: Teachers and students together engage in puzzling out 'what *it* wants you to do'" (Magdalene Lampert, "Knowing, Doing, and Teaching Multiplication," *Cognition and Instruction* 3 [1986]: 340). I suspect that Lampert is only partly correct in suggesting that this phenomenon is the result of teachers' lack of expertise in the field. Attitudes toward authority—teachers' own and those they hope to instill in students—may also play a part.

15. Eleanor Duckworth, *"The Having of Wonderful Ideas" and Other Essays on Teaching and Learning* (New York: Teachers College Press, 1987), pp. 131, 64, 6.

16. Ira Shor, *Empowering Education* (Chicago: University of Chicago Press, 1992), p. 71.

17. Herbert Simon's article, "The Structure of Ill-Structured Problems" (*Artificial Intelligence* 4 [1973]: 181–201), is cited in Norman Frederiksen, "The Real Test Bias," *American Psychologist,* March 1984, p. 199. Frederiksen invokes this distinction in order to make the point that standardized tests contain only well-structured problems, which is one reason that they tend to measure what matters least.

18. Chet Meyers, *Teaching Students to Think Critically* (San Francisco: Jossey-Bass, 1986), p. 47. "Every discipline," Meyers continues, "lends itself in some way to such an approach. There are opposing theories of mental disease, conflicting interpretations of history, different theories of management," and disagreements "about what constitutes 'real' art."

19. Another disadvantage of reading and participating in such debates is that they encourage students to accept an adversarial approach to thinking and discussing. We want them to challenge, but there's a difference between challenging in order to learn and challenging in order to win. Whenever competition is involved, learning—and ultimately the quest for truth—is apt to suffer.

20. Meier discusses these habits of mind in her book *The Power of Their Ideas* (Boston: Beacon, 1995), as well as in many of her other writings.

21. Paulo Freire, *Pedagogy of the Oppressed*, trans. Myra Bergman Ramos (1970; reprint, New York: Continuum, 1993), p. 54. Ira Shor put it this way: "All forms of education are political because they can enable or inhibit the questioning habits of students, thus developing or disabling their critical relation to knowledge, schooling, and society." Thus, "rote learning and skills drills in traditional classrooms do more than bore and miseducate students; they also inhibit their civic and emotional developments" (Shor, *Empowering Education*, pp. 12–13, 18).

22. Back before whole language became the teaching method that dare not speak its name, one survey found a .86 correlation between teachers' commitment to this approach and their liberal views on social and economic issues. That finding was reported by D. H. Creek at the 1993 meeting of the American Educational Research Association, as cited in Steven A. Stahl, "Why Innovations Come and Go (and Mostly Go): The Case of Whole Language," *Educational Researcher*, November 1999, p. 18.

23. Nel Noddings, *Happiness and Education* (Cambridge, UK: Cambridge University Press, 2003), pp. 223–24.

24. Terry Wood, "Events in Learning Mathematics: Insights from Research in Classrooms," *Educational Studies in Mathematics* 30 (1996): 86.

25. Jules Henry, *Culture Against Man* (New York: Vintage, 1963), p. 297.

26. For example, see David W. Johnson, Roger T. Johnson, and Karl A. Smith, "Academic Conflict Among Students: Controversy and Learning," in *The Social Psychology of Education*, ed. Robert S. Feldman (Cambridge, UK: Cambridge University Press, 1986); and Dean Tjosvold, "Making Conflict Productive," *Personnel Administration*, June 1984, pp. 121–30.

27. Personal communication in 1989 with Robert Deluty, a psychologist at the University of Maryland.

28. I discuss this issue in *Beyond Discipline*, rev. ed. (Alexandria, VA.: Association for Supervision and Curriculum Development, 2006), particularly in the section titled "The Value of Conflict," pp. 74–77.

29. Frank Smith, *Insult to Intelligence* (Portsmouth, NH: Heinemann, 1986), p. 201.

30. Marilyn Watson is the author of *Learning to Trust: Transforming Difficult Elementary Classrooms Through Developmental Discipline* (San Francisco: Jossey-Bass, 2003). The comments quoted here are from personal communications in 1989 and 1990.

31. This paragraph and the following one are adapted from my article "Professors Who Profess," *Kappa Delta Pi Record*, Spring 2003, pp. 108–13.

32. I can be reached at www.alfiekohn.org.

3.   Getting Hit on the Head Lessons

Suppose you have a negative reaction to a certain educational practice but you're unable to come up with any good reasons to justify your opposition. All is not lost: You can always play the "human nature" card. Never mind whether it's a good thing to help students become caring and compassionate, for example, or to work at reversing segregation. Simply assert that everyone is ultimately driven by self-interest, or that people naturally prefer to be with their own kind. Presto! All efforts to bring about change can now be dismissed as well-meaning but unrealistic.

Conversely, no logic or data are necessary when you find a practice you happen to like. Just insist that what you favor is rooted in the natural inclination of our species. A search of the *Education Week* archives reveals that various individuals have taken this tack in support of many different policies, including standardized testing ("It's just human nature that when performance is measured, performance improves") and extrinsic incentives ("Human nature . . . has always demanded, for peak performance, a potential reward consistent with effort put forth"). A lack of interest in school policies on the part of parents, a resistance to change on the part of teachers, even the practice of holding adolescent boys back a year to enhance their athletic prospects ("redshirting") have all been casually attributed to human nature.

While such assertions are never accompanied by evidence (presumably because it doesn't exist), they do prove remarkably effective at shutting down discussion. Those against whom this rhetorical ploy is used find themselves stymied because it's not easy to defend something utopian, or to oppose something unavoidable.

Here's another option for those who would rather not have to offer a substantive defense of their views: In response to a humane and respectful educational practice, they can say, "Yeah, but what's going to happen to these kids when they learn that life isn't like that?"

Invoking a dismal future, like invoking human nature, can work both ways—to attack practices one opposes and also to promote practices one prefers. I've lost track of how many times I've heard someone respond to the charge that a certain policy is destructive by declaring that children are going to experience it eventually, so they need to be prepared.

This kind of reasoning is especially popular where curriculum is concerned. Even if a lesson provides little intellectual benefit, students may have to suffer through it anyway because someone decided it will get them ready for what they're going to face in the next grade. Lilian Katz, a specialist in early childhood education, refers to this as "vertical relevance," and she contrasts it with the horizontal kind in which students' learning is meaningful to them at the time because it connects to some other aspect of their lives.

Vertical justifications are not confined to the primary grades, however. Countless middle school math teachers spend their days reviewing facts and algorithms, not because this is the best way to promote understanding or spark interest, but solely because students will be expected to know this stuff when they get to high school. Even good teachers routinely engage in bad instruction lest their kids be unprepared when more bad instruction comes their way.

In addition to forcing educators to teach too much too early, the current Tougher Standards craze has likewise emphasized a vertical rationale—in part because of its reliance on testing. Here, too, we find that "getting them ready" is sufficient reason for doing what would otherwise be seen as unreasonable. Child development experts are nearly unanimous in denouncing the use of standardized testing with young children. One Iowa principal conceded that many teachers, too, consider it "insane" to subject first graders to a four-and-a-half-hour test. However, she adds, "they need to get used to it"—an imperative that trumps all objections. In fact, why wait until first grade? A principal in California uses the identical phrase to justify testing kindergarteners: "Our philosophy is, the sooner we start giving these students tests like the Stanford 9, the sooner they'll get used to it."

What we might call the BGUTI principle—"Better Get Used To It"—is applied to other practices, too:

• Traditional grading has been shown to reduce quality of learning, interest in learning, and preference for challenging tasks. But the fact that students' efforts will be reduced to a letter or number in the future is seen as sufficient justification for giving them grades in the present.

• The available research fails to find any benefit, either academic or attitudinal, to the practice of assigning homework to elementary school students. Yet even educators who know this is true often fall back on the justification that homework—time-consuming, anxiety-provoking, and pointless though it may be—will help kids get used to doing homework when they're older. One researcher comes close to saying that the more unpleasant (and even unnecessary) the assignment, the more valuable it is by virtue of teaching children to cope with things they don't like.

• Setting children against one another in contests, so that one can't succeed unless others fail, has demonstrably negative effects—on psychological health, relationships, intrinsic motivation, and achievement—for winners and losers alike. No matter: Young children must be made to compete because—well, you get the idea.

I realize, of course, that many readers regard these practices as desirable in their own right. They may believe that competitive struggle brings out the best in children, that grading students is a constructive form of evaluation, that standardized tests accurately assess the most important aspects of learning, or that, after a full day in school, kids ought to take home more assignments regardless of whether the data show any advantage to doing so. My beef here isn't with people who hold such beliefs. It's with those who admit these practices may be damaging but defend them on BGUTI grounds.

Even if a given practice did make sense for those who are older—a very big if—that doesn't mean it's appropriate for younger children. Almost by definition, the BGUTI defense ignores developmental differences. It seems to assume that young children ought to be viewed mostly as future older children, and all children are just adults in the making. Education, in a neat reversal of Dewey's dictum, is not a process of living but merely a preparation for future living.

But the issue here isn't just preparation—it's preparation for what is unappealing. More than once, after proposing that students should participate in developing an engaging curriculum, I have been huffily informed that life isn't always interesting and kids had better learn to deal with that fact. The implication of this response seems to be that the goal of schooling is not to nourish children's excitement about learning but to get them acclimated to doing mind-numbing chores. John Holt once remarked that if people really felt that life was "nothing but drudgery, an endless list of dreary duties," one would hope they might "say, in effect, 'I have somehow missed the chance to put much joy and meaning into my own life; please educate my children so that they will do better.'"

Another example: It's common to justify rewarding and punishing students on the grounds that these instruments of control are widely used with grown-ups, too. And indeed, there are plenty of adults who do nice things only in order to receive some sort of reward, or who avoid antisocial acts just because they fear the consequence to themselves if they're caught. But are these the kinds of people we hope our kids will become?

This leads us to the most important, though rarely articulated, assumption on which BGUTI rests—that, psychologically speaking, the best way to prepare kids for the bad things they're going to encounter later is to do bad things to them now. I'm reminded of the Monty Python sketch that features Getting Hit on the Head lessons. When the student recoils and cries out, the instructor says, "No, no, no. Hold your head like this, then go, 'Waaah!' Try it again"—and gives him another smack. Presumably this is extremely useful training . . . for getting hit on the head again.

But people don't really get better at coping with unhappiness because they were deliberately made unhappy when they were young. In fact, it is experience with success and unconditional acceptance that helps one to deal constructively with later deprivation. Imposing competition or standardized tests or homework on children just because other people will do the same to them when they're older is about as sensible as saying that, because there are lots of carcinogens in the environment, we should feed kids as many cancer-causing agents as possible while they're small to get them ready.

To be sure, we don't want students to be blindsided by destructive practices with which they're completely unfamiliar (although this seems rather unlikely in our society). But how much exposure do they need? Must they spend months preparing for a standardized test to get the hang of it? Sometimes preparation can take the form of discussion rather than immersion. One need not make students compete, for example, in order to help them anticipate—and think critically about—the pervasiveness of competition in American culture.

Perhaps the preparation argument even fails on its own terms by virtue of offering a skewed account of what life is like for adults. Our culture is undeniably competitive, but cooperative skills are also valued in the workplace—and competitive schooling (spelling bees, awards assemblies, norm-referenced tests, class rank) discourages the development of those skills. Similarly, adults are more likely to be evaluated at work on the basis of how they actually do their jobs than by standardized test results. Nor, for that matter, is there much after graduation to justify the practices of same-age groupings or 50-minute periods. In short, we're not making schools for little kids more like "real life"; we're just making them more like schools for older kids.

So if these practices can't be justified as pragmatic preparation, what *is* driving BGUTI? One sometimes catches a whiff of vinegary moralism, the assumption that whatever isn't enjoyable builds character and promotes self-discipline. Mostly, though, this phenomenon may be just one more example of conservatism masquerading as realism. When children spend years doing something, they are more likely to see it as inevitable and less likely to realize that *things could be otherwise.*

"You'd better get used to it" not only assumes that life is pretty unpleasant, but that we ought not to bother trying to change the things that make it unpleasant. Rather than working to improve our schools, or other institutions, we should just get students ready for whatever is to come. Thus, a middle school whose primary mission is to prepare students for a dysfunctional high school environment soon comes to resemble that high school. Not only does the middle school fail to live up to its potential, but an opportunity has been lost to create a constituency for better secondary education. Likewise, when an entire generation comes to regard rewards and punishments, or rating and ranking, as "the way life works," rather than as practices that happen to define our society at this moment in history, their critical sensibilities are stillborn. Debatable policies are never debated. BGUTI becomes a self-fulfilling prophecy.

Finally, there is a remarkable callousness lurking just under the surface here: Your objections don't count, your unhappiness doesn't matter. Suck it up. The people who talk this way are usually on top, issuing directives, not on the bottom being directed. "Learn to live with it because there's more coming later" can be rationalized as being in the best interests of those on the receiving end, but it may just mean "Do it because I said so" and thereby cement the power of those offering this advice.

If a practice can't be justified on its own terms, then the task for children and adults alike isn't to get used to it, but to question, to challenge, and, if necessary, to resist.

Two:
The Nuts and Bolts of Learning

4. It's Not What We Teach; It's What They Learn

I never understood all the fuss about that old riddle—"If a tree falls in a forest and no one is around to hear, does it still make a sound?" Isn't it just a question of how we choose to define the word *sound?* If we mean "vibrations of a certain frequency transmitted through the air," then the answer is yes. If we mean "vibrations that stimulate an organism's auditory system," then the answer is no.

More challenging, perhaps, is the following conundrum sometimes attributed to defiant educators: "I taught a good lesson even though the students didn't learn it." Again, everything turns on definition. If teaching is conceived as an interactive activity, a process of facilitating learning, then the sentence is incoherent. It makes no more sense than "I had a big dinner even though I didn't eat anything." But what if teaching is defined solely in terms of what the teacher says and does? In that case, the statement isn't oxymoronic—it's just moronic. Wouldn't an unsuccessful lesson lead whoever taught it to ask, "So what could I have done that might have been more successful?"

That question would indeed occur to educators who regard learning—as opposed to just teaching—as the point of what they do for a living. More generally, they're apt to realize that *what we do doesn't matter nearly as much as how kids experience what we do.*

Consider what happens between children and parents. When each is asked to describe some aspect of their life together, the responses are strikingly divergent. For example, a large Michigan study that focused on the extent to which children were included in family decision making turned up different results depending on whether the parents or the children were asked. (Interestingly, three other studies found that when there is some objective way to get at the truth, children's perceptions of their parents' behaviors are no less accurate than the parents' reports of their own behaviors.)

But the important question isn't who's right; it's whose perspective predicts various outcomes. It doesn't matter what lesson a parent intended to teach by, say, giving a child a "time out" (or some other punishment). If the child experiences this as a form of love withdrawal, then that's what will determine the effect. Similarly, parents may offer praise in the hope of providing encouragement, but children may resent the judgment implicit in being informed they did a "good job," or they may grow increasingly dependent on pleasing the people in positions of authority.

From both punishments and rewards, moreover, kids may derive a lesson of conditionality: I'm loved—and lovable—only when I do what I'm told. Of course, most parents would insist that they love their children no matter what. But, as one group of researchers put it in a book about controlling styles of parenting, "It is the child's own experience of this behavior that is likely to have the greatest impact on the child's subsequent development." It's the message that's received, not the one that the adults think they're sending, that counts.

Exactly the same point applies in a school setting since educators, too, may use carrots and sticks on students. We may think we're emphasizing the importance of punctuality by issuing a detention for being late, or that we're making a statement about the need to be respectful when we suspend a student for yelling an obscenity, or that we're supporting the value of certain behaviors when we offer a reward for engaging in them.

But what if the student who's being punished or rewarded doesn't see it that way? What if his or her response is, "That's not fair!" or "Next time I won't get caught," or "I guess when you have more power, you can make other people suffer if they don't do what you want," or "If they have to reward me for x, then x must be something I wouldn't want to do."

We protest that the student has it all wrong, that the intervention really is fair, the consequence is justified, the reward system makes perfect sense. But if the student doesn't share our view, then what we did cannot possibly have the intended effect. Results don't follow from behaviors but from the meaning attached to behaviors.

The same is true of teachers who are stringent graders. Their intent—to "uphold high standards" or "motivate students to do their best"—is completely irrelevant if a low grade is perceived differently by the student who receives it, which it almost always is. Likewise, if students view homework as something they can't wait to be done with, it doesn't matter how well-designed or valuable *we* think those assignments are. The likelihood that they will help students to learn more effectively, let alone become excited about the topic, is exceedingly low.

If teachers just do their thing and leave it up to each student to make sense of it—"so that the child comes to feel, as he is intended to, that when he doesn't understand, it is his fault" (to borrow John Holt's words)—then meaningful learning is likely to be in awfully short supply in those classrooms.

But let's face it: It's easier to concern yourself with teaching than with learning, just as it's more convenient to say the fault lies with people other than you when things go wrong. It's tempting, when students are given some kind of assessment, to assume the results primarily reveal how much progress each kid is, or isn't, making—rather than noticing that the quality of the teaching is also being assessed.

"I taught a good lesson . . ." probably suggests that learning is viewed as a process of absorbing information, which in turn means that teaching consists of delivering that information. (Many years ago, the writer George Leonard described lecturing as the "best way to get information from teacher's notebook to student's notebook without touching the student's mind.") This approach is particularly common among high school and college teachers, who have been encouraged to think of themselves as experts in their content areas (literature, science, history) rather than in pedagogy. The *reductio ad absurdum* would be those who "took their content so very seriously that they forgot their students," as Linda McNeil put it in her devastating portrait of high school.

The trouble may start in schools of education, where preservice teachers in many states spend very little time learning about learning, relative to the time devoted to subject-matter content. Worse, when teachers these days *are* told to think about learning, it may be construed in behaviorist terms, with an emphasis on discrete, measurable skills. The point isn't to deepen understanding (and enthusiasm) but merely to elevate test scores.

The fact is that real learning often can't be quantified, and a corporate-style preoccupation with "data" turns schooling into something shallow and lifeless. Ideally, attention to learning signifies an effort to capture how each student makes sense of the world so we can meet them where they are. "Teaching," as Deborah Meier reminded us, "is mostly listening." (It's the learners, she added, who should be doing most of the "telling," based on how they grapple with an engaging curriculum.) Imagine how American classrooms would be turned inside out if we ever really put that wisdom into action.

And it's not just listening in the literal sense that's needed but the willingness to imagine the student's point of view. How does it feel to be sitting there with your shaky efforts to write an essay or solve a problem subjected to continuous evaluation? (Many teachers who expect their students to bear up under, and even benefit from, a constant barrage of criticism are themselves often extremely sensitive to any suggestion that their craft could be improved.) Indeed, educators ought to make a point of trying something new in their own lives, something they must struggle to master, in order to appreciate what their students put up with every day.

Finally, as teachers are to students, so administrators are to teachers. Successful school leadership doesn't depend on what principals and superintendents do, but on how their actions are regarded by *their* audience—notably, classroom teachers. Those on the receiving end may be older, but the moral is the same: It's best to see what we do through the eyes of those to whom it's done.

5.   Who's Cheating Whom?

An article about cheating practically writes itself. It must begin, of course, with a shocking statistic or two to demonstrate the pervasiveness of the problem, perhaps accompanied by a telling anecdote or a quotation from a shrugging student ("Well, sure, everyone does it"). This would be followed by a review of different variants of unethical behavior and a look at who is most likely to cheat. Finally, a list of ideas must be provided for how we can deter or catch cheaters, along with a stern call for greater vigilance.

Just about everyone agrees that cheating is bad and that we need to take steps to prevent it. But it is precisely this overwhelming consensus that makes me uneasy. Whenever a conclusion seems so obvious and is accepted so uncritically, it's probably time to take a fresh look. That doesn't mean we're obligated to give equal time to arguments in favor of cheating, but it may make sense to reconsider what the term actually signifies and examine what leads students to do what they're not supposed to—and what that tells us about their schooling.

In the 1970s, a social psychologist at Stanford University named Lee Ross attracted some attention (at least within his field) by coining the term "fundamental attribution error." He defined this as a tendency to "underestimate the impact of situational factors and to overestimate the role of dispositional factors in controlling behavior."[1] Ross was summarizing what a number of experiments had already demonstrated: We frequently pay so much attention to character, personality, and individual responsibility that we overlook how profoundly the social environment affects what we do and who we are.

There are surely examples of this error to be found everywhere, but it may be particularly prevalent in a society where individualism is both a descriptive reality and a cherished ideal. We Americans are stubbornly resistant to the simple truth that another eminent social psychologist, Philip Zimbardo, recently summarized in a single sentence: "Human behavior is more influenced by things outside us than inside."[2] Specifically, we're apt to assume that people who commit crimes are morally deficient, that the have-nots in our midst are lazy (or at least insufficiently resourceful), that children who fail to learn simply aren't studying hard enough (or have unqualified teachers). In other words, we treat each instance of illegality, poverty, or academic difficulty as if it had never happened before and as if the individual in question was acting out of sheer perversity or incompetence.

Cheating is a case in point because most discussions of the subject focus on—which is to say, attribute the problem to—the cheaters themselves. The dominant perspective on the issue, as educational psychologist Bruce Marlowe recently remarked, "is all about 'Gotcha!'"[3] This continues to be true even though we've known for quite some time that the environment matters at least as much as individual character when trying to predict the occurrence of various types of cheating. Nearly 80 years ago, in a study that has come to be regarded as a classic work of social science, a group of researchers at Teachers College, Columbia University, investigated almost 11,000 children between the ages of eight and sixteen over a period of five years and found that "even slight changes in the situation affect individual behavior in unpredictable ways." As a result, the correspondence between what any given child would do in two different circumstances was "lower than would be required for accurate prediction of individual behavior." Cheating, the researchers concluded, "is as much a function of the particular situation in which [the student] is placed as it is of his own inner experience and training, his general ideas and ideals, his fears, ambition, and purposes."[4]

A fair amount of research has accumulated since the publication of that report to illuminate the situations in which students *are* most likely to cheat and to help us understand the reasons they do so. We've learned, first of all, that when teachers don't seem to have a real connection with their students, or when they don't seem to care much about them, students are more inclined to cheat.[5] That's a very straightforward finding, and not a particularly surprising one, but if taken seriously, it has the effect of shifting our attention and reshaping the discussion.

So, too, does a second finding: Cheating is more common when students experience the academic tasks they've been given as boring, irrelevant, or overwhelming. In two studies of ninth and tenth graders, for example, "Perceived likelihood of cheating was uniformly relatively high . . . when a teacher's pedagogy was portrayed as poor."[6] To put this point positively, cheating is relatively rare in classrooms where the learning is genuinely engaging and meaningful to students and where a commitment to exploring significant ideas hasn't been eclipsed by a single-minded emphasis on "rigor." The same is true in "democratic classes where [students'] opinions are respected and welcomed."[7] List the classroom practices that nourish a disposition to find out about the world, the teaching strategies that are geared not to covering a prefabricated curriculum but to *dis*covering the significance of ideas, and you will have enumerated the conditions under which cheating is much less likely to occur. (Interestingly, one of the mostly forgotten findings from that old Teachers College study was that "progressive school experiences are less conducive to deception than conventional school experiences"—a result that persisted even after the researchers controlled for age, IQ, and family background. In fact, the more time students spent in either a progressive school or a traditional school, the greater the difference between the two in terms of cheating.)[8]

Third, "when students perceive that the ultimate goal of learning is to get good grades, they are more likely to see cheating as an acceptable, justifiable behavior," as one group of researchers summarized their findings in 2001.[9] Cheating is particularly likely to flourish if schools use honor rolls and other incentives to heighten the salience of grades, or if parents offer financial inducements for good report cards[10]—in other words, if students are not merely rewarded for academic success, but are also rewarded for being rewarded.

Grades, however, are just the most common manifestation of a broader tendency on the part of schools to value product more than process, results more than discovery, achievement more than learning. If students are led to focus on how well they're doing more than on *what* they're doing, they may do whatever they think is necessary to make it look as though they're succeeding. Thus, a recent study of more than 300 students in two California high schools confirmed that the more classrooms drew attention to students' academic performance, the more students "observed and engaged in various types of cheating."[11]

The goal of acing a test, getting a good mark, making the honor roll, or impressing the teacher is completely different from—indeed, antithetical to—the goal of figuring out what makes some objects float and some sink or why the character in that play we just read is so indecisive. When you look at the kind of schooling that's all about superior results and "raising the bar," you tend to find a variety of unwelcome consequences:[12] less interest in learning for its own sake, less willingness to take on challenging tasks (since the point is to produce good results, not to take intellectual risks), more superficial thinking . . . and more cheating.

That is exactly what Eric Anderman, a leading expert on the subject, and his colleagues have found. In a 1998 study of middle school students, those who "perceived that their schools emphasized performance [as opposed to learning] goals were more likely to report engaging in cheating behaviors." Six years later, he turned his attention to the transition from eighth to ninth grade and looked at the culture of individual classrooms. The result was essentially the same: More cheating took place when teachers emphasized good grades, high test scores, and being smart. There was less cheating when they made it clear that the point was to enjoy the learning, when understanding mattered more than memorizing, and when mistakes were accepted as a natural result of exploration.[13] Interestingly, these studies found that even students who acknowledged that it's wrong to cheat were more likely to do so when the school culture placed a premium on results.

It makes perfect sense when you think about it. Cheating can help you to get a good grade and look impressive (assuming you don't get caught), so it's a strategy that might well appeal to students with those goals. But it would be pointless to cheat if you were interested in the learning itself because cheating can't help you understand an idea.[14] How, then, do students *develop* certain goals? What leads them to display an interest in what they're doing as opposed to a concern about how well they're doing it? Individual dispositions count for something; obviously all students don't behave identically even in the same environment. But that environment—the values and policies of a classroom, a school, or a society—is decisive in determining how pervasive cheating will be.[15] It affects students' behaviors at the moment and shapes their values and attitudes over time. What the data are telling us, like it or not, is that cheating is best understood as a symptom of problems with the priorities of schools and the practices of educators. To lose sight of that fact by condemning the kids who cheat and ignoring the context is to fall into the trap that Lee Ross warned us about.

One major cause of cheating, then, is an academic environment in which students feel pressured to improve their performance even if doing so involves methods that they, themselves, regard as unethical. But when you look carefully at the research that confirms this discovery, you begin to notice that the worst environments are those in which the pressure is experienced in terms of one's standing *relative to others.*

Competition is perhaps the single most toxic ingredient to be found in a classroom, and it is also a reliable predictor of cheating. Grades are bad enough, for example, but the practice of grading on a curve—or ranking students against one another—is much worse. Similarly, while it's destructive to lean on students to raise their test scores, it's even more damaging to lead them to think about how their scores compare to those of other students (in another school or another country). And while using rewards to "motivate" people is generally counterproductive,[16] the negative effects are intensified with *a*wards—which is to say, the practice of making rewards (or recognition) artificially scarce so that students must try to triumph over one another.

Competitive schools are those where, by design, all students cannot succeed. To specify the respects in which that arrangement is educationally harmful may help us understand its connections to cheating. Competition typically has an adverse impact on relationships because each person comes to look at everyone else as obstacles to his or her own success. Competition often contributes to a loss of intrinsic motivation because the task itself, or the act of learning, becomes a means to an end—the end being victory. (Competition may "motivate" some people, but only in the sense of supplying an extrinsic inducement; at best this fails to promote interest in the task, but more often interest in the task actually diminishes.) Competition often erodes academic self-confidence (even for winners)—partly because students come to think of their competence as dependent on how many people they've beaten and partly because the dynamics of competition really do interfere with the development of higher-order thinking.[17] In each case, cheating becomes more likely, as students feel unsupported, uninterested, and incompetent, respectively.

In short, a competitive school is to cheating as a warm, moist environment is to mold—except that in the latter case we don't content ourselves with condemning the mold spores for growing. Moreover, competition is the ultimate example of focusing on performance rather than on learning, so it's no wonder that "cheating qualifies as part of the unhealthy legacy that results from having tied one's sense of worth to achieving competitively," as the eminent psychologist Martin Covington explained. In an early investigation, he heard echoes of this connection from the students themselves. One told him, "Kids don't cheat because they are bad. They are afraid that they aren't smart and what will happen if they don't do good." Another said that students who cheat "feel really bad but it is better than being yelled at for bad grades." And from a third: "People cheat because they are afraid of doing poorer than other kids and feeling miserable for being different and behind. Some do it to be the best in class or move to the next group."[18] How ironic, then, that some of the adults who most vociferously deplore cheating also support competitive practices—and confuse competitiveness with excellence—with the result that cheating is more likely to occur.

Because competition, a relentless focus on achievement, and bad pedagogy aren't new, it stands to reason that cheating isn't exactly a recent development either. The Teachers College group had no shortage of examples to study. In fact, Elliot Turiel compared surveys of students from the 1920s with those conducted today and found that about the same percentage admitted to cheating in both eras—an interesting challenge to those who view the past through a golden haze and seem to take a perverse satisfaction in thinking of our times as the worst ever.[19]

But let's assume for a moment that the alarmists are right. If it's true that cheating, or at least some versions of it, really is at an all-time high, that may well be because pressures to achieve are increasing, competitiveness is more rampant and virulent, and there is a stronger incentive to cut corners or break rules. In fact, we're currently witnessing just such pressures not only on children but on teachers and administrators who are placed in an environment where everything depends on their students' standardized test scores.[20]

If schools focus on relative achievement and lead students to do the same, it may be because they exist in a society where education is sometimes conceived as little more than a credentialing ritual. Schools then become, in the words of educational historian David Labaree, "a vast public subsidy for private ambition," places where "self-interested actors [seek] opportunities for gaining educational distinctions at the expense of each other." And if the point is just to get ahead, he continues, individuals may seek "to gain the highest grade with the minimum amount of learning."[21] Cheating could be seen as a rational choice in a culture of warped values.

A deep analysis of cheating may lead us to investigate not only the situations that give rise to it but the process by which we come to decide what will be classified as cheating in the first place. Even a careful examination of the social context usually assumes that cheating, almost by definition, is unethical. But perhaps things are more complicated. If cheating is defined as a violation of the rules, then we'd want to know whether those rules are reasonable, who devised them, and who stands to benefit by them. Yet these questions are rarely asked.

Some kinds of cheating involve actions that are indisputably objectionable. Plagiarism is one example. While it's not always clear in practice where to draw the line between an idea that has been influenced by the work of other writers and one that clearly originated with someone else (and ought to be identified as such),[22] we should be able to agree that it's wrong to use a specific concept or a verbatim passage from another source without giving credit if the objective is to deceive the reader about its origin.[23] More interesting, though, and perhaps just as common, are those cases where what is regarded as cheating actually consists of a failure to abide by restrictions that may be arbitrary and difficult to defend. It's not just that questionable educational practices may *cause* students to cheat, in other words; it's that such practices are responsible for *defining* certain behaviors as cheating. In the absence of those practices and the ideology supporting them, such behaviors would not be regarded as illegitimate.

This unsettling possibility enjoys a prima facie plausibility because there are plenty of other things we regard as facts of life whose existence actually turns out to be dependent on social context. Sportsmanship, for example, is an artificial concept that wouldn't exist at all except for competition: Only in activities where people are attempting to defeat one another is it meaningful to talk about doing so in a graceful or virtuous fashion. (People who play cooperative games don't require reminders to be "good sports" because they're working *with* one another toward a common goal.) Likewise, theft does not exist in cultures where there is no private property—not because people refrain from stealing but because the idea literally has no meaning if people's possessions are not off-limit to one another. There is no such thing as leisure unless work is experienced as alienating or unfulfilling. You cannot commit blasphemy unless you believe there is a God to be profaned. And jaywalking is a meaningless concept in Boston, where I live, because there is simply no expectation that pedestrians should cross only at intersections.

On what, then, does the concept of cheating depend for *its* existence? One answer was supplied by a scandal at the Massachusetts Institute of Technology in the early 1990s. More than seventy students were punished for "cheating" because they worked in small groups to write computer programs for fear that they would otherwise be unable to keep up with their class assignments. "Many feel that the required work is clearly impossible to do by straightforward"—that is, solitary—"means," observed the faculty member who chaired MIT's Committee on Discipline.[24] The broader context in which to understand this episode is that cooperative learning, beyond helping students deal with an overwhelming workload, also provides a number of benefits when compared with individual or competitive instructional models. By working together, students not only are able to exchange information and divide up tasks but typically end up engaging in more sophisticated problem-solving strategies, which, in turn, results in more impressive learning on a range of measures. Structured cooperation in the classroom also proves beneficial in terms of self-esteem, relationships, and motivation to learn.[25]

The problem, however, is that, aside from the occasional sanctioned group project, the default condition in most American classrooms—particularly where homework and testing are concerned—is reflected in that familiar injunction heard from elementary school teachers: "I want to see what *you* can do, not what your neighbor can do." (Or, if the implications were spelled out more precisely, "I want to see what you can do all by yourself, deprived of the resources and social support that characterize most well-functioning real-world environments, rather than seeing how much more you and your neighbors could accomplish together.") Whether, and under what circumstances, it might make more sense to have students learn, and to assess their performance, in groups is an issue ripe for analysis and disagreement. Alas, most collaboration is simply classified as cheating. End of discussion.

By the same token, students may be disciplined if they consult reference sources during any sort of assessment in which the teacher has forbidden this. But what does it say about the instructor, and the education system, that assessment is geared largely to students' ability to memorize? What pedagogical purpose is served by declaring that students will be judged on this capacity and must therefore spend a disproportionate amount of time attempting to cram dates, definitions, and other facts into their short-term memories? How else might we have encouraged them to spend that time? And what is the purpose of this sort of assessment? Is information being collected about students' capacity to remember what they've read or heard for the purpose of helping them to learn more effectively— or is the exercise more about sorting them (comparing students to one another) or controlling them (by using assessment to elicit compliance)?

It may well be that students who use "unauthorized" materials or assistance thereby compromise the teacher's preferred method of assessment. But perhaps this should lead us to question the legitimacy of that plan and ask why those materials have been excluded. Similarly, if "cheating hinders standardization," as one group of academics warned,[26] should we condemn the cheaters or question the value of a standardized education? Again, we can expect lively debate on these questions; but again, what is troubling is the absence of such debate—the result of uncritically accepting conventional definitions and assumptions. Consulting a reference source during an exam (or working with one's peers on an assignment) will be classified as cheating in one classroom, with all the grave implications and practical repercussions attendant on that label, while it will be seen as appropriate, even admirable, in another. Students unlucky enough to find themselves in the first classroom stand condemned of cheating, with little attention paid to the nature of the rules they broke. To that extent, *their actions have violated a purely* conventional *set of prohibitions but they are treated as though guilty of a* moral *infraction.*

Moreover, any student who offered just such a defense, perhaps arguing that her action was actually less problematic than the instructor's requirements, or that what she did was more analogous to entering a lecture hall through a door marked "exit" than to lying or stealing, would likely be accused of engaging in denial, attempting to displace responsibility for what she has done, or trying to rationalize her behavior. Once we've decided that someone's action is morally wrong, her efforts to challenge that premise, no matter how well reasoned, merely serve to confirm our view of her immorality.

In 2006, a front-page story in the *New York Times* described how instructors and administrators are struggling to catch college students who use ingenious high-tech methods of cheating. In every example cited in the article, the students were figuring out ways to consult their notes during exams; in one case, a student was caught using a computer spell-check program. The implication here, which is that students even at the university level are being tested primarily on their capacity to memorize, was noted neither by the reporter nor by any of his sources. Only a single sentence dealt with the nature of the assessments: "Several professors said they tried to write exams on which it was hard to cheat, posing questions that outside resources would not help answer."[27] Even here, the intent appeared to be foiling cheaters rather than improving the quality of assessment and instruction. Or, to put it differently, the goal was to find ways to prevent students from being *able* to cheat rather than addressing the reasons they *wanted* to cheat—or what the instructors *regarded* as cheating (and why).

These distinctions are important. An Alabama student, quoted in another article, pointed out that "you can cheat if all you are going to be tested on are facts, but it is much harder to cheat when you are asked to . . . write an essay." However, this student went on to make a much more significant point: "Maybe a bigger problem is that teachers require students to memorize instead of teaching them how to think."[28] The deficiencies of the curriculum, in other words, go well beyond whether they facilitate or discourage cheating.

Dudley Barlow, a retired high school teacher and education

columnist, recalled assigning a research paper about El Salvador. One student began with some facts about the country

> and then went on to describe how General William Booth and his band of followers worked diligently to help the downtrodden by spreading the gospel of Christ. I was absolutely stumped about the paper until I realized the student had sat in a library copying from an encyclopedia about El Salvador, and he had inadvertently turned two pages at one time. Without even realizing it, he began copying text about the Salvation Army.

This story presents us with a kind of projective test, notable for what our reactions to it reveal about us. It's not just that some will be appalled and others will find it funny; it's that some will regard it as a reflection on the student, while others will zero in on what the teacher had assigned the student (and his classmates) to do. Fortunately, Barlow himself had the courage to adopt the latter point of view. "That student," he concluded, "finally convinced me that the kinds of research papers I had customarily assigned were not accomplishing what I had in mind."[29] What he had in mind, presumably, was helping students to learn as well as to take pleasure in doing so. And detecting or deterring cheating more effectively, as one language arts teacher explains, fails to address the "educational damage" caused by whatever systemic forces have taught students that "the final product takes precedence over learning."[30]

Thus, suppose that cheating could be at least partly curtailed by tightly monitoring and regulating students or by repeatedly announcing the dire penalties that await anyone who breaks the rules. Would this result be worth the cost of creating a climate of mistrust, undermining a sense of community, and perhaps leading students to become less enthusiastic about learning? Rebecca Moore Howard, who teaches writing at Syracuse University, put it this way: "In our stampede to fight what some call a 'plague' of plagiarism, we risk becoming the enemies rather than the mentors of our students; we are replacing the student-teacher relationship with the criminal-police relationship. . . . Worst of all, we risk not recognizing that our own pedagogy needs reform . . . [if it] encourages plagiarism because it discourages learning."[31]

It is sometimes said that students who take forbidden shortcuts with their homework will just end up "cheating themselves" because they will not derive any intellectual benefits from doing the assignment. This assertion, too, is often accepted on faith rather than prompting us to ask just how likely it is that the assignment really would prove valuable if it had been completed in accordance with instructions. A review of the available evidence on the effects of homework fails to support widely held beliefs about its benefits.[32] To that extent, we're forced to confront the possibility that students' violation of the instructor's rules not only may fail to constitute a moral infraction but also may not lead to any diminution of learning. Outraged condemnations of cheating, at least in such instances, may turn out to have more to do with power than with either ethics or pedagogy. Perhaps what actually elicits that outrage is not a lack of integrity on the part of students so much as a lack of conformity.[33]

A penetrating analysis of cheating will at least raise these possibilities, even if it may not always lead to these conclusions. It will invite us to re-examine what comes to be called cheating and to understand the concept as a function of the context in which the label is used. Even if the reality of cheating is unquestioned, however, its causes will lead us to look at the actions of teachers as well as the (re)actions of students, and at classroom and cultural structures as well as individual behaviors. Such a perspective reminds us that how we educate students is the dog; cheating is just the tail.

Notes

1. Lee Ross, "The Intuitive Psychologist and His Shortcomings: Distortions in the Attribution Process," in *Advances in Experimental Social Psychology*, vol. 10, ed. Leonard Berkowitz (New York: Academic Press, 1977), p. 183.
2. Philip Zimbardo, quoted in Claudia Dreifus, "Finding Hope in Knowing the Universal Capacity for Evil," *New York Times*, April 3, 2007, p. D-2.

3. Marlowe teaches at Roger Williams University in Rhode Island. Personal communication, August 2006.

4. Character Education Inquiry, *Studies in the Nature of Character,* vol. 1: *Studies in Deceit* (New York: Macmillan, 1928), book 1, pp. 381, 400.

5. See the research conducted with undergraduates and high school students by Gregory Schraw, Lori Olafson, Fred Kuch, Trish Lehman, Stephen Lehman, and Matthew T. McCrudden, "Interest and Academic Cheating," in *Psychology of Academic Cheating,* eds. Eric M. Anderman and Tamera B. Murdock (Burlington, MA: Elsevier Academic Press, 2007).

6. Tamera B. Murdock, Angela Miller, and Julie Kohlhardt, "Effects of Classroom Context Variables on High School Students' Judgments of the Acceptability and Likelihood of Cheating," *Journal of Educational Psychology* 96 (2004): 775. Also see the research reviewed by Schraw et al., pp. 60–65.

7. This finding by Kay Johnston at Colgate University was described in Lynley H. Anderman, Tierra M. Freeman, and Christian E. Mueller, "The 'Social' Side of Social Context: Interpersonal and Affiliative Dimensions of Students' Experiences and Academic Dishonesty," in *Psychology of Academic Cheating,* eds. Anderman and Murdock, p. 207.

8. Character Education Inquiry, *Studies in the Nature of Character,* book 2, p. 184.

9. This paraphrase of a conclusion by Rutgers professor Donald McCabe and his colleagues in an article called "Cheating in Academic Institutions: A Decade of Research," is offered by Eric M. Anderman, "The Effects of Personal, Classroom, and School Goal Structures on Academic Cheating," in *Psychology of Academic Cheating,* eds. Anderman and Murdock, p. 95.

10. Schraw et al., "Interest and Academic Cheating," p. 69.

11. Jason M. Stephens and Hunter Gehlbach, "Under Pressure and Underengaged: Motivational Profiles and Academic Cheating in High School," in *Psychology of Academic Cheating,* eds. Anderman and Murdock. Quotation appears on p. 127. Also see the review of other research in Anderman, "The Effects of Personal, Classroom, and School Goal Structures on Academic Cheating."

12. For more on the research behind this distinction and the detrimental effects of overemphasizing academic performance, see Alfie Kohn, *The Schools Our Children Deserve: Moving Beyond Traditional Classrooms and "Tougher Standards"* (Boston: Houghton Mifflin, 1999), chapter 2.

13. Eric M. Anderman, Tripp Griesinger, and Gloria Westerfield, "Motivation and Cheating During Early Adolescence," *Journal of Educational Psychology* 90 (1998): 84–93; and Eric M. Anderman and Carol Midgley, "Changes in Self-Reported Academic Cheating Across the Transition from Middle

School to High School," *Contemporary Educational Psychology* 29 (2004): 499–517.

14. On this point, see Anderman, "The Effects of Personal, Classroom, and School Goal Structures on Academic Cheating," p. 93.

15. For example, see Anderman et al., "Motivation and Cheating During Early Adolescence"; and Angela D. Miller, Tamera B. Murdock, Eric M. Anderman, and Amy L. Poindexter, "Who Are All These Cheaters? Characteristics of Academically Dishonest Students," in *Psychology of Academic Cheating*, eds. Anderman and Murdock, p. 20.

16. Alfie Kohn, *Punished by Rewards: The Trouble with Gold Stars, Incentive Plans, A's, Praise, and Other Bribes*, rev. ed. (Boston: Houghton Mifflin, 1999).

17. Alfie Kohn, *No Contest: The Case Against Competition*, rev. ed. (Boston: Houghton Mifflin, 1992).

18. Martin Covington, *Making the Grade: A Self-Worth Perspective on Motivation and School Reform* (Cambridge, UK: Cambridge University Press, 1992), p. 91.

19. See Susan Gilbert, "Scientists Explore the Molding of Children's Morals," *New York Times*, March 18, 2003, p. D-5.

20. For an excellent review of the prevalence of, reasons for, and moral ambiguity surrounding cheating by educators in the context of high-stakes testing, see Sharon L. Nichols and David C. Berliner, *Collateral Damage: How High-Stakes Testing Corrupts America's Schools* (Cambridge, MA: Harvard Education Press, 2007), especially chapter 2. Also see Thomas M. Haladyna, Susan Bobbit Nolen, and Nancy S. Haas, "Raising Standardized Achievement Test Scores and the Origins of Test Pollution," *Educational Researcher* 20, no. 5 (June-July 1991): 2–7; and Claudia Kolker, "Texas Offers Hard Lessons on School Accountability," *Los Angeles Times*, April 14, 1999.

21. David F. Labaree, *How to Succeed in School Without Really Learning: The Credentials Race in American Education* (New Haven: Yale University Press, 1997), pp. 258, 32, 259.

22. "Encouraged by digital dualisms, we forget that plagiarism means many different things: downloading a term paper, failing to give proper credit to the source of an idea, copying extensive passages without attribution, inserting someone else's phrases or sentences—perhaps with small changes—into your own prose, and forgetting to supply a set of quotation marks. If we ignore these distinctions, we fail to see that most of us have violated the plagiarism injunctions in one way or another, large or small, intentionally or inadvertently, at one time or another. The distinctions are just not that crisp" (Rebecca Moore Howard, "Forget About Policing Plagiarism. Just *Teach*," *Chronicle of Higher Education*, November 16, 2001, p. B-24).

23. The intent to deceive is critical because plagiarism is sometimes unconscious. It's not uncommon for people to borrow someone else's work while

genuinely believing it's their own. In fact, this happens often enough that it's been given a name ("cryptomnesia") and become a subject for social psychological research. See, for example, Alan S. Brown and Dana R. Murphy, "Cryptomnesia: Delineating Inadvertent Plagiarism," *Journal of Experimental Psychology: Learning, Memory, and Cognition* 15 (1989): 432–42; and Jesse Preston and Daniel M. Wegner, "The Eureka Error: Inadvertent Plagiarism by Misattributions of Effort," *Journal of Personality and Social Psychology* 92 (2007): 575–84.

24. Quoted in Fox Butterfield, "Scandal over Cheating at M.I.T. Stirs Debate on Limits of Teamwork," *New York Times,* May 22, 1991, p. A-23.

25. For example, see the research reviewed in *Cooperation and Competition: Theory and Research,* David W. Johnson and Roger T. Johnson (Edina, MN: Interaction Books, 1989); and in Kohn, *No Contest.* For a recent meta-analysis of the effects of cooperative learning and peer tutoring in elementary school, see Marika D. Ginsburg-Block, Cynthia A. Rohrbeck, and John W. Fantuzzo, "A Meta-Analytic Review of Social, Self-Concept, and Behavioral Outcomes of Peer-Assisted Learning," *Journal of Educational Psychology* 98 (2006): 732–49.

26. Linda Garavalia, Elizabeth Olson, Emily Russell, and Leslie Christensen, "How Do Students Cheat?" in *Psychology of Academic Cheating,* eds. Anderman and Murdock, p. 35.

27. Jonathan D. Glater, "Colleges Chase as Cheats Shift to Higher Tech," *New York Times,* May 18, 2006, pp. A-1, A-24.

28. This student is quoted in Paris S. Strom and Robert D. Strom, "Cheating in Middle School and High School," *Educational Forum,* Winter 2007, p. 112.

29. Dudley Barlow, "Cut, Paste, and Get Caught: Plagiarism and the Internet," *Education Digest,* May 2006, p. 40.

30. Lisa Renard, "Cut and Paste 101: Plagiarism and the Net," *Educational Leadership,* December 1999/January 2000, p. 41.

31. Howard, "Forget About Policing Plagiarism."

32. Alfie Kohn, *The Homework Myth: Why Our Kids Get Too Much of a Bad Thing* (Cambridge, MA: Da Capo Press, 2006).

33. The same motive appears to be on display when students who clearly have mastered the material in a course are nevertheless given a lower grade because they failed to complete all the homework. Here the student has implicitly disconfirmed the hypothesis that homework is necessary for successful learning, and the teacher responds by saying, in effect, that the point isn't to learn so much as it is to do what one is told.

6. How to Create Nonreaders: Reflections on Motivation, Learning, and Sharing Power

Autonomy-supportive teachers seek a student's initiative . . . whereas controlling teachers seek a student's compliance.

—JOHNMARSHALL REEVE, ELIZABETH BOLT, AND YI CAI

Not that you asked, but my favorite Spanish proverb, attributed to the poet Juan Ramón Jiménez, can be translated as follows: "If they give you lined paper, write the other way." In keeping with this general sentiment, I'd like to begin my contribution to an issue of *English Journal* whose theme is "Motivating Students" by suggesting that it is impossible to motivate students.

In fact, it's not really possible to motivate anyone, except perhaps yourself. If you have enough power, sure, you can make people, including students, do things. That's what rewards (e.g., grades) and punishments (e.g., grades) are for. But you can't make them do those things well—"You can command writing, but you can't command good writing," as Donald Murray once remarked—and you can't make them *want* to do those things. The more you rely on coercion and extrinsic inducements, as a matter of fact, the less interest students are likely to have in whatever they were induced to do.

What a teacher *can* do—*all* a teacher can do—is work with students to create a classroom culture, a climate, a curriculum that will nourish and sustain the fundamental inclinations that everyone starts out with: to make sense of oneself and the world, to become increasingly competent at tasks that are regarded as consequential, to connect with (and express oneself to) other people. Motivation—at least intrinsic motivation—is something to be supported, or if necessary revived. It's not something we can instill in students by acting on them in a certain way. You can tap their motivation, in other words, but you can't "motivate them." And if you think this distinction is merely semantic, then I'm afraid we disagree.

On the other hand, what teachers clearly have the ability to do with respect to students' motivation is kill it.[1] That's not just a theoretical possibility; it's taking place right this minute in too many classrooms to count. So, still mindful of the imperative to "write the other way," I'd like to be more specific about how a perversely inclined teacher might effectively destroy students' interest in reading and writing. I'll offer six suggestions without taking a breath, and then linger on the seventh.

Seven Ways to Kill Students' Motivation
1. Quantify their reading assignments.

Nothing contributes to a student's interest in (and proficiency at) reading more than the opportunity to read books that he or she has chosen. But it's easy to undermine the benefits of free reading. All you need to do is stipulate that students must read a certain number of pages, or for a certain number of minutes, each evening. When they're told how *much* to read, they tend to just "turn the pages" and "read to an assigned page number and stop," says Christopher Ward Ellsasser, a California high school teacher.[2] And when they're told how *long* to read—a practice more common with teachers of younger students—the results are not much better. As Julie King, a parent, reports, "Our children are now expected to read 20 minutes a night, and record such on their homework sheet. What parents are discovering (surprise) is that those kids who used to sit down and read for pleasure—the kids who would get lost in a book and have to be told to put it down to eat/play/whatever—are now setting the timer . . . and stopping when the timer dings. . . . Reading has become a chore, like brushing your teeth."

2. Make them write reports.

Jim DeLuca, a middle school teacher, summed it up: "The best way to make students hate reading is to make them prove to you that they have read. Some teachers use log sheets on which the students record their starting and finishing page for their reading time.

Other teachers use book reports or other projects, which are all easily faked and require almost no reading at all. In many cases, such assignments make the students hate the book they have just read, no matter how they felt about it before the project."[3]

3. Isolate them.

I've been in the same book group for twenty-five years. We read mostly fiction, both classic and contemporary, at the rate of almost a book a month. I shudder to think how few novels I would have read over that period, and how much less pleasure (and insight) I would have derived from those I did manage to read, without the companionship of my fellow readers. Many teachers are familiar with literature circles and other ways of helping students to create a community of readers. You'd want to avoid such innovations—and have kids read (and write) mostly on their own—if your goal were to cause them to lose interest in what they're doing.

4. Focus on skills.

Children grow to love reading when it's about making meaning, when they're confronted directly by provocative ideas, compelling characters, delicious prose. But that love may never bloom if all the good stuff is occluded by too much attention to the machinery—or, worse, the approved vocabulary for describing that machinery. Knowing the definition of dramatic irony or iambic pentameter has the same relationship to being literate that memorizing the atomic weight of nitrogen has to doing science. When I look back on my brief career teaching high school English, I think I would have been far more successful had I asked fewer questions that have only one correct answer. I should have helped the kids to dive headfirst into the realm of metaphor rather than wasting their time on how a metaphor differs from a simile. "School teaches that literacy is about a set of skills, not a way to engage a part of the world," as Eliot Washor, Charles Mojkowski, and Deborah Foster recently wrote. "Consequently, many young people come to associate reading with schooling rather than with learning more about what interests them."[4]

5. Offer them incentives.

Scores of studies have confirmed that rewards tend to lead people to lose interest in whatever they had to do to snag them. This principle has been replicated with many different populations (across genders, ages, and nationalities) and with a variety of tasks as well as different kinds of inducements (money, A's, food, and praise, to name four).[5] You may succeed in getting students to read a book by dangling a reward in front of them for doing so, but their interest in reading, per se, is likely to evaporate—or, in the case of kids who have little interest to begin with, is unlikely to take root—because you've sent the message that reading is something one wouldn't *want* to do. (Duh. If it was fun, why would they be bribing me to do it?) Elaborate commercial programs (think Accelerated Reader or Book It!) may be the most efficient way to teach kids that reading isn't pleasurable in its own right, but ordinary grades will do just as well in a pinch. As far as I can tell, every single study that has examined grades and intrinsic motivation has found that the former has a negative effect on the latter.[6]

6. Prepare them for tests.

Just as a teacher's grade can be every bit as effective at killing motivation as imported incentive programs, so a teacher's quiz can hold its own against your state's standardized exam. It's not the test itself that does the damage; it's what comes before. Heidegger said that life is lived toward—informed by and in anticipation of—death (*Sein zum Tode*). By analogy, a classroom where learning is always pointed to a test (*Lernen zum Examen?*) is one where ideas, and the act of reading, are experienced as just so many means to an end. That, of course, is exactly the same effect that rewards create, so if your classroom is one that emphasizes tests *and* grades, the damage is effectively doubled. And if those tests and grades are mostly focused on memorizing facts and mastering mechanical skills, well, you've won the Triple Crown at creating a roomful of nonreaders.

7. Restrict their choices.

Teachers have less autonomy these days than ever before. The predominant version of school reform, with its emphasis on "accountability" and its use of very specific curriculum standards enforced by tests, proceeds from the premise that teachers need to be told what, and how, to teach. At the same time, this movement confuses excellence with uniformity ("All students in ninth grade will . . . ") and with mere difficulty (as if that which is more "rigorous" were necessarily better). It's now reaching its apotheosis with an initiative to impose the same core standards on every public school classroom in the nation. This effort has been sponsored primarily by corporate executives, politicians, and test manufacturers, but, shamefully, a number of education organizations have failed to take a principled stand in opposition. Instead, they have eagerly accepted whatever limited role in the design of standards they're permitted by the corporate sponsors, thereby giving the impression that this prescriptive, one-size-fits-all approach to schooling enjoys legitimacy and the support of educators. The bigger picture here, which transcends and predates national standards, features top-down control all the way along the education food chain, from legislators and state school officials to school boards to superintendents to principals to teachers. That means the pivotal question for teachers—a moral as well as a practical question—is whether they will treat students the way they, themselves, are being treated . . . or the way they *wish* they were being treated.

Those who choose the latter course—a "working with" approach—make a point of bringing students into the process of making decisions whenever possible. Teachers who choose the former—a "doing to" approach—may, as I say, be taking their cue from the management style of those who seek to micromanage *them*. Then again, they may be reproducing the teacher-centered classrooms with which they're familiar. Or perhaps they just find it difficult to give up control. As long-time educators Harvey Daniels and Marilyn Bizar put it rather provocatively, "Teachers probably wouldn't have originally chosen their vocation if they didn't crave the spotlight on some deep psychological level. The hunger to 'really teach something' has probably derailed more student-centered innovations than administrative cowardice and textbook company co-option combined."[7]

Mea culpa. When I taught, almost every classroom decision was made unilaterally by me: what students would read, in what format they would respond to the readings, how their learning would be assessed, how much time would be devoted to a book or topic, whether a given task would be done in small groups or as a whole class, how conflicts would be resolved, whether homework was really necessary (and, if so, what would be assigned and when it would be due), how the chairs were arranged and what was posted on the walls. To be honest, it never occurred to me to ask rather than to tell. After all, it was my classroom, wasn't it?

Well, yes, it was, but not because it had to be—only because I kept all the power to myself. And my students were the poorer for it. The sad irony is that as children grow older and become more capable of making decisions, they're given less opportunity to do so in schools. In some respects, teenagers actually have less to say about their learning—and about the particulars of how they'll spend their time in school each day—than do kindergartners. Thus, the average American high school is excellent preparation for adult life . . . assuming that one lives in a totalitarian society.

When parents ask, "What did you do in school today?" kids often respond, "Nothing." Howard Gardner pointed out that they're probably right, because "typically school is *done to* students."[8] This sort of enforced passivity is particularly characteristic of classrooms where students are excluded from any role in shaping the curriculum, where they're on the receiving end of lectures and questions, assignments and assessments. One result is a conspicuous absence of critical, creative thinking—something that (irony alert!) the most controlling teachers are likely to blame on the students themselves, who are said to be irresponsible, unmotivated, apathetic, immature, and so on. But the fact is that kids learn to make good decisions by making decisions, not by following directions.

Conversely, students who have almost nothing to say about what happens in class are more likely to act out, tune out, burn out, or simply drop out. Again, it takes some courage to face the fact that these responses are related to what *we're* doing, or not doing. And the same is true of my larger point in this essay: A lack of opportunity to make decisions may well manifest itself in a lack of interest in reading and writing. Were that our goal, our single best strategy might be to run a traditional teacher-centered, teacher-directed classroom.

Supporting Students' Desire to Learn

At this point, I'll abandon the somewhat labored conceit of showing you how to kill interest and instead try to suggest, in more straightforward fashion, some ways to think about how students can play a more active role in their own learning. My assumption is that if you've read this far, you'd probably like to support their desire to learn and read. First, then, a few general principles.

1. Supporting their autonomy isn't just about having them pick this over that.

"The experience of self-determination is not something that can be given to the student through the presentation of an array of teacher-determined options (e.g., 'Here are six books; which do you want to read today?')."[9] I think there are two insights here. The first is that deeper learning and enthusiasm require us to let students *generate* possibilities rather than just choose items from our menu; construction is more important than selection. The second is that what we really need to offer is "autonomy support," an idea that's psychological, not just pedagogical. It's derived from a branch of psychology called self-determination theory, founded by Edward Deci and Richard Ryan, among others. To support students' autonomy is to meet their need to be in control of their own lives, to offer opportunities to decide along with the necessary guidance and encouragement, to "minimiz[e] the salience of evaluative pressure and any sense of coercion in the classroom" and "maximiz[e] students' perceptions of having a voice and choice."[10]

In 1993 I wrote about the advantages of offering voice and choice, detailing how students benefited intellectually, morally, and psychologically, according to the available research.[11] Since then, the data have continued to accumulate. Two experts in the field offered this summary in 2006:

Empirical research has shown that students with autonomy-supportive teachers, compared with students with controlling teachers, experience not only greater perceived autonomy, but also more positive functioning in terms of their classroom engagement, emotionality, creativity, intrinsic motivation, psychological well-being, conceptual understanding, academic achievement, and persistence in school.[12]

2. Autonomy can be supported—and choices can be made—collectively.

While it is surely important for students to be able to make some decisions that apply only to themselves, many more opportunities should be available for the class to figure out things together. In fact, one might say that when autonomy and community are combined, they define a concept more often invoked than practiced in our society: democracy.

Even during the absurdly short class periods still being used in most high schools, it makes sense to devote some of that limited time to class meetings in which students can solve problems and make decisions. I once sat in on several classes taught by Keith Grove at Dover-Sherborn High School near Boston and noticed that such meetings were critical to his teaching; he had come to realize that the feeling of community (and active participation) they produced made whatever time remained for the explicit curriculum far more productive than devoting the whole period to talking at rows of silent kids. Together, the students decided whether to review the homework in small groups or as a whole class. Together, they decided when it made sense to schedule their next test. (After all, what's the point of assessment—to have students show you what they know when they're ready to do so, or to play "gotcha"?) Interestingly, Grove says that his classes are quite structured even though they're unusually democratic, and he sees his job as being "in control of putting students in control."[13]

3. It's not all or nothing.

Teachers who favor a traditional approach to teaching sometimes offer a caricature of an autonomy-supportive classroom—one devoid of intellectual challenge where kids do whatever they feel like—in order to rationalize rejecting this model. But autonomy support not only doesn't exclude structure, as Keith Grove reminds us; it also doesn't rule out active teacher involvement. That involvement can be direct, such as when teacher and students negotiate a mutually acceptable due date for an essay. (Instead of "You folks choose," it may be "Let's figure this out together.") Or the involvement can be indirect, with the teacher setting up broad themes for the course and students making decisions within those parameters. But that doesn't mean we should be prepared to share power with students only about relatively minor issues. It may make sense to start with that and then challenge ourselves to involve them in thinking about bigger questions as you (and they) become more comfortable with a democratic classroom.

4. "See above."

The half-dozen suggestions for killing interest in reading in the first part of this essay don't become irrelevant just because students are given more authority to direct their learning, individually and collectively. For example, rewards are still counterproductive even if kids get to choose what goodie they'll get. And there's reason to worry if a language arts course is focused mostly on narrowly defined facts and skills even if students are permitted to make decisions about the details. (As one of Bianca's suitors observes in *The Taming of the Shrew*, "There's small choice in rotten apples.") Even autonomy support in its richest sense works best in the context of a course that's pedagogically valuable in other ways—and avoids various familiar but counterproductive practices.

Concrete Ideas

Finally, here are a few specific suggestions for bringing students in on making decisions, offered here in the hope that they will spark you to think of others in the same spirit:

• Let students sample a work of literature, then generate their own questions and discussion topics—for themselves and one another.

• Before having students help each other to revise their writing, invite them to brainstorm possible questions they might ask about its construction and its impact on the reader (rather than having them simply apply *your* editing guidelines or, worse, evaluating the writing against a prefabricated rubric).[14]

• Have students think together about ideas for the papers they'll write, then follow up once the writing is underway by inviting each student to ask the group for suggestions. Encourage discussion about the rationale for, and usefulness of, each idea that emerges in order to promote reflection that may well benefit everyone.

• When you're planning to respond to their journals or other writings, begin by asking students—individually and as a class—what kinds of responses would be most helpful to them. (Wouldn't you prefer that administrators proceed that way when offering feedback on your teaching?)

• Let students choose the audience for whom they're writing, as well as the genre in which they respond to something they've read (e.g., play, op-ed, speech).

• Check in periodically with students during class meetings about how the course is going for them, whether the decision-making process seems to be working, whether the climate is conducive to learning. Ask what might make discussions and assignments more productive and satisfying—but only if you're really open to making changes based on what they tell you.

• Bring students in on the process of assessment by asking them to join you in thinking about alternatives to conventional tests. "How can you show me what you understood, where you still need help, and what *I* may need to rethink about how I taught the unit?" Beyond the format of the assessment, invite them as a class to suggest criteria by which someone's work might be evaluated—and, later, have them apply those criteria to what they've done.

• Remember that group decision making doesn't require voting, which is basically just adversarial majoritarianism. Help them to acquire the skills and disposition to reach for a deeper kind of democracy, one in which compromises are generated and consensus is reached.

Giving Up Control

To be willing to give up some control is to avoid getting too invested in the amazing course you designed. Strive to take pleasure and pride from how you help students to learn and become excited about learning, not just from the curriculum itself. Even the most thoughtful lesson, the cleverest assignment, the richest reading list is much less likely to goose students and engage them and help them to think more subtly, if you came up with it on your own and imposed it *on* them. What matters is not what we teach; it's what they learn, and the probability of real learning is far higher when the students have a lot to say about both the content and the process.

The best teachers, I find, spend at least some of their evenings smacking themselves on the forehead—figuratively, at least—as they reflect on something that happened during the day. "Why did *I* decide that, when I could have asked the kids?" And, thinking about some feature of the course yet to come: "Is this a choice I should be making for the students rather than with them?" One Washington, D.C., creative writing teacher was pleased with himself for announcing to students that it was up to them to decide how to create a literary magazine—until he realized later that he had incrementally reasserted control. "I had taken a potentially empowering project and turned it into a showcase of what [I] could do."[15] It takes insight and guts to catch oneself at what amounts to an exercise in pseudodemocracy. Keeping hold of power—overtly for traditionalists, perhaps more subtly for those of us who think of ourselves as enlightened progressives—is a hell of a lot easier than giving it away.

But if we're serious about helping students to fall in love with literature, to get a kick out of making words fall together in just the right order, then we have to be attentive to what makes these things more, and less, likely to happen. It may take us awhile, but ultimately our classrooms should turn the usual default setting on its head so the motto becomes: Let the students decide except when there's a good reason why we have to decide for them.

Notes

1. The management theorist Frederick Herzberg made an analogous argument about the asymmetrical motivational properties of money in the workplace: Just because paying people too little can be demotivating doesn't mean that paying them more will elicit greater satisfaction or more motivation to do their best. This helps to explain why pay-for-performance plans are doomed to fail.

2. All uncited quotations, like this one, are derived from personal communications.

3. Regie Routman invites us to imagine ourselves on the receiving end of such assignments: "Think about the last time you read a book you loved. Imagine how you would have felt if you had been required to write a book report or a summary that had to include the main idea and supporting details. Or, if at the end of chapters, you'd been required to write answers to questions. For myself, that would have been enough to turn me off to reading the book"; *Literacy at the Crossroads* (Portsmouth, NH: Heinemann, 1996), p. 177.

4. Elliot Washor, Charles Mojkowski, and Deborah Foster, "Living Literacy," *Phi Delta Kappan*, March 2009, p. 522.

5. See Edward L. Deci, Richard Koestner, and Richard M. Ryan, "A Meta-analytic Review of Experiments Examining the Effects of Extrinsic Rewards on Intrinsic Motivation," *Psychological Bulletin* 125 (1999): 627–68; and my book *Punished by Rewards* (Boston: Houghton Mifflin, 1993).

6. I review some of this research, as well as studies that find a detrimental effect of grades on quality of learning and preference for challenge, in *Punished by Rewards* and *The Schools Our Children Deserve* (Boston: Houghton Mifflin, 1999), as well as in "From Degrading to De-Grading," *High School Magazine*, March 1999, pp. 38–43, which is available at www.alfiekohn.org/teaching/fdtd-g.htm.

7. Harvey Daniels and Marilyn Bizar, *Methods That Matter* (York, ME: Stenhouse, 1998), p. 12.

8. Howard Gardner, *The Unschooled Mind* (New York: Basic, 1991), p. 243.

9. Johnmarshall Reeve, Glen Nix, and Diane Hamm, "Testing Models of the Experience of Self-Determination in Intrinsic Motivation and the Conundrum of Choice," *Journal of Educational Psychology* 95 (2003): 388.

10. Christopher P. Niemic and Richard M. Ryan, "Autonomy, Competence,

and Relatedness in the Classroom: Applying Self-Determination Theory to Educational Practice," *Theory and Research in Education* 7 (2009): 139. For an argument that "cognitive autonomy support" may be more important for student engagement with learning than "procedural" or "organizational" autonomy support, see Candice R. Stefanou, Kathleen C. Perencevich, Matthew DiCintio, and Julianne C. Turner, "Supporting Autonomy in the Classroom: Ways Teachers Encourage Student Decision Making and Ownership," *Educational Psychologist* 39 (2004): 98–110.

11. See Alfie Kohn, "Choices for Children: Why and How to Let Students Decide," *Phi Delta Kappan*, September 1993, pp. 8–20, which is available at www.alfiekohn.org/teaching/cfc.htm.

12. Johnmarshall Reeve and Hyungshim Jang, "What Teachers Say and Do to Support Students' Autonomy During a Learning Activity," *Journal of Educational Psychology* 98 (2006): 210. Many of these effects were confirmed in a large meta-analysis published two years later; see Erika A. Patall, Harris Cooper, and Jorgianne Civey Robinson, "The Effects of Choice on Intrinsic Motivation and Related Outcomes: A Meta-Analysis of Research Findings," *Psychological Bulletin* 134 (2008): 270–300.

13. Kohn, "Choices for Children."

14. On this last point, see Maja Wilson, *Rethinking Rubrics in Writing Assessment* (Portsmouth, NH: Heinemann, 2006); and Kohn, "The Trouble with Rubrics," which appears as chapter 7 in this volume.

15. Sami Miranda, "Yours, Mine, or Ours?" *Rethinking Schools*, Summer 1999, p. 10.

7.   The Trouble with Rubrics

Once upon a time, I vaguely thought of assessment in dichotomous terms: The old approach, which consisted mostly of letter grades, was crude and uninformative, while the new approach, which included things like portfolios and rubrics, was detailed and authentic. Only much later did I look more carefully at the individual floats rolling by in the alternative assessment parade—and stop cheering.

For starters, I realized that it's hardly sufficient to recommend a given approach on the basis of its being better than old-fashioned report cards. By that criterion, just about anything would look good. I eventually came to understand that not all alternative assessments are authentic. My growing doubts about rubrics in particular were prompted by the assumptions on which this technique rested and also the criteria by which they (and assessment itself) were typically judged. These doubts were stoked not only by murmurs of dissent I heard from thoughtful educators but by the case made *for* this technique by its enthusiastic proponents. For example, I read in one article that "rubrics make assessing student work quick and efficient, and they help teachers to justify to parents and others the grades that they assign to students."[1] To which the only appropriate response is: Uh-oh.

First of all, something that's commended to teachers as a handy strategy of self-justification during parent conferences ("Look at all these 3's, Mrs. Grommet! How could I have given Zach anything but a B?") doesn't seem particularly promising for inviting teachers to improve their practices, let alone rethink their premises.

Second, I'd been looking for an alternative to grades because research shows three reliable effects when students are graded: They tend to think less deeply, avoid taking risks, and lose interest in the learning itself.[2] The ultimate goal of authentic assessment must be the elimination of grades. But rubrics actually help to *legitimate* grades by offering a new way to derive them. They do nothing to

   Originally published in *English Journal*, March 2006

address the terrible reality of students who have been led to focus on getting A's rather than on making sense of ideas.

Finally, there's the matter of that promise to make assessment "quick and efficient." I've graded enough student papers to understand the appeal here, but the best teachers would react to that selling point with skepticism, if not disdain. They'd immediately ask what we had to sacrifice in order to spit out a series of tidy judgments about the quality of student learning. To ponder that question is to understand how something that presents itself as an innocuous scoring guide can be so profoundly wrongheaded.

Consistent and uniform standards are admirable, and maybe even workable, when we're talking about, say, the manufacture of DVD players. The process of trying to gauge children's understanding of ideas is a very different matter, however. It necessarily entails the exercise of human judgment, which is an imprecise, subjective affair. Rubrics are, above all, a tool to promote standardization, to turn teachers into grading machines or at least allow them to pretend that what they're doing is exact and objective. Frankly, I'm amazed by the number of educators whose opposition to standardized tests and standardized curricula mysteriously fails to extend to standardized in-class assessments.

The appeal of rubrics is supposed to be their high interrater reliability, finally delivered to language arts. A list of criteria for what should be awarded the highest possible score when evaluating an essay is supposed to reflect near-unanimity on the part of the people who designed the rubric and is supposed to assist all those who use it to figure out (that is, to discover rather than to decide) which essays meet those criteria.

Now some observers criticize rubrics because they can never deliver the promised precision; judgments ultimately turn on adjectives that are murky and end up being left to the teacher's discretion. But I worry more about the success of rubrics than their failure. Just as it's possible to raise standardized test scores as long as you're willing to gut the curriculum and turn the school into a test-preparation factory, so it's possible to get a bunch of people to agree on what rating to give an assignment as long as they're willing to accept and apply someone else's narrow criteria for what merits that rating. Once we check our judgment at the door, we can all learn to give a 4 to exactly the same things.

This attempt to deny the subjectivity of human judgment is objectionable in its own right. But it's also harmful in a very practical sense. In an important article published in 1999, Linda Mabry, now at Washington State University, pointed out that rubrics "are designed to function as scoring guidelines, but they also serve as arbiters of quality and agents of control" over what is taught and valued. Because "agreement among scorers is more easily achieved with regard to such matters as spelling and organization," these are the characteristics that will likely find favor in a rubricized classroom. Mabry cites research showing that "compliance with the rubric tended to yield higher scores but produced 'vacuous' writing."[3]

To this point, my objections assume only that teachers rely on rubrics to standardize the way they think about student assignments. Despite my misgivings, I can imagine a scenario where teachers benefit from consulting a rubric briefly in the early stages of designing a curriculum unit in order to think about various criteria by which to assess what students end up doing. As long as the rubric is only one of several sources, as long as it doesn't drive the instruction, it could conceivably play a constructive role.

But all bets are off if *students* are given the rubrics and asked to navigate by them. The proponent I quoted earlier, who boasted of efficient scoring and convenient self-justification, also wants us to employ these guides so that students will know ahead of time exactly how their projects will be evaluated. In support of this proposition, a girl who didn't like rubrics is quoted as complaining, "If you get something wrong, your teacher can prove you knew what you were supposed to do."[4] Here we're invited to have a good laugh at this student's expense. The implication is that kids' dislike of these things proves their usefulness.

Just as standardizing assessment for teachers may compromise the quality of teaching, so standardizing assessment for learners may compromise the learning. Mindy Nathan, a Michigan teacher and former school board member told me that she began "resisting the rubric temptation" the day "one particularly uninterested student raised his hand and asked if I was going to give the class a rubric for this assignment." She realized that her students, presumably grown accustomed to rubrics in other classrooms, now seemed "unable to function unless every required item is spelled out for them in a grid and assigned a point value. Worse than that," she added, "they do not have confidence in their thinking or writing skills and seem unwilling to really take risks."[5]

This is the sort of outcome that may not be noticed by an assessment specialist who is essentially a technician, in search of practices that yield data in ever-greater quantities. A B+ at the top of a paper tells a student very little about its quality, whereas a rubric provides more detailed information based on multiple criteria. Therefore, a rubric is a superior assessment.

The fatal flaw in this logic is revealed by a line of research in educational psychology showing that students whose attention is relentlessly focused on how well they're doing often become less engaged with *what* they're doing. There's a big difference between thinking about the content of a story you're reading (for example, trying to puzzle out why a character made a certain decision), and thinking about your own proficiency at reading. "Only extraordinary education is concerned with learning," the writer Marilyn French once observed, whereas "most is concerned with achieving: and for young minds, these two are very nearly opposites."[6] In light of this distinction, it's shortsighted to assume that an assessment technique is valuable in direct proportion to how much information it provides. At a minimum, this criterion misses too much.

But the news is even worse than that. Studies have shown that too much attention to the quality of one's performance is associated with more superficial thinking, less interest in whatever one is doing, less perseverance in the face of failure, and a tendency to attribute the outcome to innate ability and other factors thought to be beyond one's control.[7] To that extent, more detailed and frequent evaluations of a student's accomplishments may be downright counterproductive. As one sixth grader put it, "The whole time I'm writing, I'm not thinking about what I'm saying or how I'm saying it. I'm worried about what grade the teacher will give me, even if she's handed out a rubric. I'm more focused on being correct than on being honest in my writing."[8] In many cases, the word *even* in that second sentence might be replaced with *especially*. But, in this respect at least, rubrics aren't uniquely destructive. Any form of assessment that encourages students to keep asking, "How am I doing?" is likely to change how they look at themselves and at what they're learning, usually for the worse.

What all this means is that improving the design of rubrics, or inventing our own, won't solve the problem because the problem is inherent to the very idea of rubrics and the goals they serve. This is a theme sounded by Maja Wilson in her extraordinary new book, *Rethinking Rubrics in Writing Assessment.*[9] In boiling "a messy process down to 4–6 rows of nice, neat, organized little boxes," she argues, assessment is "stripped of the complexity that breathes life into good writing." High scores on a list of criteria for excellence in essay writing do not mean that the essay is any good because quality is more than the sum of its rubricized parts. To think about quality, Wilson argues, "we need to look to the piece of writing itself to suggest its own evaluative criteria"—a truly radical and provocative suggestion.

Wilson also makes the devastating observation that a relatively recent "shift in writing pedagogy has not translated into a shift in writing assessment." Teachers are given much more sophisticated and progressive guidance nowadays about how to teach writing but are still told to pigeonhole the results, to quantify what can't really be quantified. Thus, the dilemma: Either our instruction and our assessment remain "out of synch" or the instruction gets worse in order that students' writing can be easily judged with the help of rubrics.

Again, this is not a matter of an imperfect technique. In fact, when the how's of assessment preoccupy us, they tend to chase the why's back into the shadows. So let's shine a light over there and ask: What's our *reason* for trying to evaluate the quality of students' efforts? It matters whether the objective is to (1) rank kids against one another, (2) provide an extrinsic inducement for them to try harder, or (3) offer feedback that will help them become more adept at, and excited about, what they're doing. Devising more efficient rating techniques—and imparting a scientific luster to those ratings—may make it even easier to avoid asking this question. In any case, it's certainly not going to shift our rationale away from (1) or (2) and toward (3).

Neither we nor our assessment strategies can be simultaneously devoted to helping all students improve *and* to sorting them into winners and losers. That's why we have to do more than reconsider rubrics. We have to reassess the whole enterprise of assessment, the goal being to make sure it's consistent with our motivation for wanting to be teachers.

Notes

1. Heidi Goodrich Andrade, "Using Rubrics to Promote Thinking and Learning," *Educational Leadership,* February 2000, p. 13.

2. I review this research in *Punished by Rewards: The Trouble with Gold Stars, Incentive Plans, A's, Praise, and Other Bribes* (Boston: Houghton Mifflin, 1993) and *The Schools Our Children Deserve: Moving Beyond Traditional Classrooms and "Tougher Standards"* (Boston: Houghton Mifflin, 1999), as well as in "From Degrading to De-Grading," *High School Magazine,* March 1999, pp. 38–43.

3. Linda Mabry, "Writing to the Rubric," *Phi Delta Kappan,* May 1999, pp. 678, 676.

4. Quoted by Andrade, "Understanding Rubrics," in http://learnweb.harvard.edu/alps/thinking/docs/rubricar.htm. Another educator cites this same quotation and adds: "Reason enough to give rubrics a closer look!" It's also quoted on the RubiStar Web site, which is a sort of online rubric-o-matic.

5. Mindy Nathan, personal communication, October 26, 2004. As a student teacher, Nathan was disturbed to find that her performance, too, was evaluated by means of a rubric that offered a ready guide for evaluating instructional "competencies." In an essay written at the end of her student-

teaching experience, she commented, "Of course, rubrics don't lie; they just don't tell the whole story. They crunch a semester of shared learning and love into a few squares on a sheet that can make or break a career." That's why she vowed, "I won't do this to my students. My goal as a teacher will be to preserve and present the human aspects of my students that defy rubricization."

6.   Marilyn French, *Beyond Power: On Women, Men, and Morals* (New York: Summit, 1985), p. 387.

7.   For more on the distinction between performance and learning—and the detrimental effects of an excessive focus on performance—see *The Schools Our Children Deserve*, chapter 2, which reviews research by Carol Dweck, Carole Ames, Carol Midgley, John Nicholls, and others.

8.   Quoted in Natalia Perchemlides and Carolyn Coutant, "Growing Beyond Grades," *Educational Leadership*, October 2004, p. 54. Notice that this student is actually making two separate points. Even some critics of rubrics, who are familiar with the latter objection—that honesty may suffer when technical accuracy is overemphasized—seem to have missed the former one.

9.   Maja Wilson, *Rethinking Rubrics in Writing Assessment* (Portsmouth, NH: Heinemann, 2006).

Three: Climate & Connections
How Does School Feel to the Students?

8.   The Value of Negative Learning

I recently spent a delightful few hours devouring twenty-seven auto-biographical essays written by alternative educators from around the world. Collectively, these people had founded schools, magazines, and entire movements, helping to promote all manner of nontraditional learning. What fascinated me was that only one of them had attended an alternative school himself. All the others had somehow become committed to a progressive, democratic, or child-centered approach in spite of having experienced something very different as a student. Or *because of* having experienced something very different as a student.

When we stop to think about what we were made to do in school, we may recall grumbling about all the stuff that was clearly point-less—or worse. But at the same time, being children, we tended to accept it all as so many facts of life: the schedule, the rules, the curriculum, the adults who were downright mean. We may not have liked it, just as we didn't much care for unpleasant weather, but hey, whatcha gonna do?

What's far more discouraging is that, even as adults, many people never manage to acquire a sense of perspective, a recognition that Things Could Have Been Otherwise, along with the attendant outrage—or at least indignation. They never correct that child's posture of passive acceptance, never come to see school policies as contingent, manmade, opposable. It doesn't occur to them to question the premise that when kids do something bad, something bad must be done to them. They never think to ask whether it's necessary to make children begin a second shift of working on academic tasks once they get home from a full day in school. They take on faith that a child's learning must be reduced to a letter or number rating, and that most classroom time should be spent listening instead of doing.

In fact, lots of people grow up and subject their own children to the same kind of schooling that they themselves barely endured.

Some of these parents do so with enthusiasm (and flash cards), which is alarming; others just resign themselves to the inevitability of watching their children act out an excruciating slow-motion exercise in déjà vu, which is even worse. Apparently their mantra is: "If it was bad enough for me, it's bad enough for my kids."

So how is it that some folks emerge with an understanding that traditional education is unhealthy for children and other living things, *and* with some insight about why that's true (and what might make more sense instead), *and* with a commitment to show the rest of us a better way? How did they get here from there?

I suspect the key is a phenomenon that might be called "negative learning," in which people regard an unfortunate situation as a chance to figure out what *not* to do. They sit in awful classrooms and pay careful attention because they know they're being exposed to an enormously useful anti-model. They say to themselves, "Here is someone who has a lot to teach me about how not to treat children." Some people perfect this art of negative learning while they're still in those environments; others do it retrospectively, questioning what was done to them earlier even if they never thought—or were unable—to do so before. Some people do it on their own; others need someone to lend them the lens that will allow them to look at things that way.

Of course, a mind-numbing, spirit-killing school experience doesn't reliably launch people into self-actualization, intellectual curiosity, or a career in alternative education. If it did, we'd want everyone to live through that. Nontraditional educators had to beat the odds, and they've set themselves the task of improving those odds for other children, creating places where the learning doesn't have to be by negative example.

I want new teachers to see progressive education at its best. I want them to spend as much time as possible in a place where they can watch seasoned educators work *with* children rather than doing things *to* them, helping those children to make sense of ideas and create opportunities to discover answers to their own questions, striving to shield them from stultifying mandates handed down from on high. It's hard enough to walk into a classroom on wobbly legs and face a roomful of students for the first time; if at all possible, you want to have had a few caring role models who take intellectual inquiry—and kids—seriously.

But if apprentice teachers find themselves instead in a place where test scores drive the instruction and students are essentially bullied into doing whatever they're told, then it helps to be able to think, "What a memorable display of lousy pedagogy and disrespect for children! I need to take careful notes so, when it's my turn, I can do *exactly the opposite.*" Again, they'll need plenty of help: People can't just will themselves into being proficient progressive teachers. Still, construing a bad classroom as an opportunity for negative learning may jump-start the process, and the same trick can help people who are forced to deal with autocratic administrators, arrogant advisors, or even abusive parents.

How do some among us manage to perform this heuristic alchemy, adopting a constructive mental set even though others who are similarly situated end up just feeling lousy about themselves and about education? My hunch is that it reflects a confluence of environment and personality. Maybe the environment has to be really dreadful, as opposed to merely dull—but at the same time must include a glimpse of something better so it's clear what's missing. People need to know from experience that schools or teachers or families don't *have* to be like this.

The personality part, meanwhile, probably should include equal measures of assertiveness (including a contrarian spirit and a dash of up-yours rebelliousness) and empathy. The contribution of the former is obvious, but the latter is no less important. Some people suffer through the indignity or even brutality of being a newbie somewhere—a fraternity, a medical residency, whatever—and then, once they've attained a little seniority, turn around and abuse the new arrivals. They may derive a certain satisfaction from watching others suffer. They may even convince themselves that having been treated like dirt was somehow good for them. (Beware of anyone who rationalizes and reproduces emotional violence with phrases like "character building" or "tough love.")

But other people—the ones we're looking for—are those who

say, "I want to work to change this system so others will be spared what was done to me." They have the compassion and the courage to shake up the status quo and denounce cruel traditions. They've mastered the art of negative learning and developed a commitment to making the world, or at least whatever part of it they come to inhabit, a better place than it was before they got there.

9.   Unconditional Teaching

Has there even been a wider, or more offensive, gap between educational rhetoric and reality than that which defines the current accountability fad? The stirring sound bites waft through the air: higher expectations . . . world-class standards . . . raising the bar . . . no child left behind. Meanwhile, educators and students down on the ground are under excruciating pressure to improve test results, often at the expense of meaningful learning, and more low-income and minority students are dropping out.

Some of the results of that pressure are plainly visible to anyone who cares to look: You can see practice tests replacing student-designed projects, children appearing alternately anxious and bored, terrific teachers quitting in disgust. But there are also subtler effects. The current version of school reform is changing what we value. If the sole goal is to raise achievement (in the narrowest sense of that word), then we may end up ignoring other kinds of learning beyond the academic. It's exceedingly difficult to teach the whole child when people are held accountable only for raising reading and math scores.

Moreover, when some capabilities are privileged over others, and a broader approach to education is sacrificed, we begin to look at students differently. We come to lose sight of children "except as they distribute themselves across deciles."[1] That means that some kids—namely, the high scorers—are prized more than others by the adults. One Florida superintendent observed that "when a low-performing child walks into a classroom, instead of being seen as a challenge, or an opportunity for improvement, for the first time since I've been in education, teachers are seeing [him or her] as a liability."[2] I've heard essentially the same rueful observation from teachers and administrators across the country.

Debilitating Effects of Conditional Acceptance

A diminution in *what* we value, then, may affect *whom* we value. But the damage isn't limited to those students who fail to measure up—that is, by conventional standards. If some children matter more to us than others, then all children are valued only conditionally. Regardless of the criteria we happen to be using, or the number of students who meet those criteria, every student gets the message that our acceptance is never a sure thing. They learn that their worth hinges on their performance.

That's more than distasteful—it's debilitating. Psychological theorists and researchers are coming to realize that the best predictor to mental health may not be one's level of self-esteem but the extent to which it fluctuates.[3] The real problem isn't self-esteem that's too low ("I don't like myself very much") so much as self-esteem that's too contingent ("I like myself only when . . . "). Conversely, kids who have an underlying sense of their own value are more likely to see failure as a temporary setback, a problem to be solved. They're also less likely to be anxious or depressed.[4]

In turn, the best predictor of whether children will be able to accept themselves as fundamentally valuable and capable is the extent to which they have been accepted unconditionally by others. As Carl Rogers argued half a century ago,[5] those on the receiving end of conditional love—that is, affection based not on who they are but on what they do—come to disown the parts of themselves that aren't valued. Eventually they regard themselves as worthy only when they act (or think or feel) in specific ways.

In the course of researching a book on these issues, I discovered considerable empirical support for this theory. One summary of the research put it this way: "The more conditional the support [one experiences], the lower one's perceptions of overall worth as a person."[6] When children receive affection with strings attached, they do indeed tend to accept themselves only with strings attached. For example, investigators at the University of Denver have shown that teenagers who feel they have to fulfill certain conditions in order to win their parents' approval often end up not liking themselves. That, in turn, may lead a given adolescent to construct a "false self"—in other words, to pretend to be the kind of person whom his or her parents *will* love. This desperate strategy to gain acceptance is often associated with depression, a sense of hopelessness, and a tendency to lose touch with one's true self. At some point, such teenagers may not even know who they really are because they've had to work so hard to become something they're not.[7]

In short, unconditional acceptance is what kids require in order to flourish. And while it's most critical that they experience that kind of acceptance at home, what happens at school matters, too. "Unconditional parenting"[8] is key, but what might be called "unconditional teaching" is also important. One study found that students who felt unconditionally accepted by their teachers were more likely to be genuinely interested in learning and to enjoy challenging academic tasks—as opposed to just doing things because they had to and preferring easier assignments at which they knew they would be successful.[9]

To provide this unconditional support, we must actively oppose the policies that get in the way, such as those that encourage us to value children on the basis of their academic standing—or, worse, merely on the basis of their test scores. Although there are risks involved, there may well be a moral obligation to participate in organized, active resistance to destructive mandates. "Putting children first" is an empty slogan if we watch passively while our schools are turned into test-prep centers.

Taking a stand against oppressive policies that are imposed from outside our schools may well be a necessary component of unconditional teaching, but it's not sufficient. Even if we succeeded in eliminating external pressures related to standards and testing, it's possible that some of our own practices also lead children to believe that we accept them only conditionally. Sometimes that acceptance seems to depend on their doing well and sometimes it depends on their being good. Let's look at each of these in turn.

Acceptance Based on Performance

All of us want our students to be successful learners, but there is a thin line that separates valuing excellence (a good thing) from leading students to believe that they matter only to the extent they meet our standards (not a good thing). Some people elevate abstractions like Achievement or Excellence above the needs of flesh-and-blood children. Thus, by steering extra resources to, or heaping public recognition on, students who succeed, we're not only ignoring the counterproductive effects of extrinsic motivators,[10] but possibly sending a message to all students—those who have been recognized and those who, conspicuously, have not—that only those who do well count.

Nel Noddings made a similar point in discussing the kind of teacher who pushes students relentlessly but also praises those who manage to live up to his high expectations ("You are the best!"). Such instructors are often admired for being both demanding and encouraging. However, if "You are the best!" just means "You can do A.P. calculus," then this suggests that only those who master differential equations are "the best." Surely, says Noddings, "a student should not have to succeed at A.P. calculus to gain a math teacher's respect."[11]

Or consider those educators, particularly in the arts, whose professional pride is invested in the occasional graduate who goes on to distinguish herself as a well-known novelist or violinist. There is a big difference between trying to help as many students as possible cultivate a love of, and some competence at, one's field and trying to sift through many hundreds of students in search of the very few who will later become famous. The latter suggests a profoundly antidemocratic sensibility, one that sees education as being about winnowing and selecting rather than providing something of value for everyone. And, again, all students realize that they matter to such a teacher only if they measure up.

My point is not that we shouldn't value, or even celebrate, accomplishment. But paradoxically, unconditional teaching is more likely to create the conditions for children to excel. Those who know they're valued irrespective of their accomplishments often end up accomplishing quite a lot. It's the experience of being accepted without conditions that helps people develop a healthy confidence in themselves, a belief that it's safe to take risks and try new things.

Acceptance Based on Obedience

Sometimes the conditions placed on acceptance have more to do with compliance than with success. A case in point: temporarily ejecting a student from a class activity—or even from school—for misbehaving. This practice is sometimes rationalized on the grounds that it isn't fair to the others if one student is allowed to act badly. But those other students, the ones in whose name we are allegedly taking this action, are being told, in effect, that everyone is part of this community only conditionally. That creates an uneasy, uncertain, and ultimately unsafe climate.

Adele Faber and Elaine Mazlish ask us to put ourselves in the place of a child who has been subjected to the punishment known euphemistically as time-out: "As an adult you can imagine how resentful and humiliated you would feel if someone forced you into isolation for something you said or did." For a child, however, it is even worse, since she may come to believe "that there is something so wrong with her that she has to be removed from society."[12]

Those who seem to accept students conditionally—requiring them to act in a particular way in order to be valued, or even in order to be allowed to stay—often see themselves as trying to reinforce or eliminate specific student behaviors. What they often don't see is that traditional classroom management techniques, along with the narrow emphasis on observable behaviors that underlies those techniques, make it very difficult to attend to the person who engages in those behaviors. In fact, I would propose the following rule of thumb: The value of a book about dealing with children is inversely proportional to the number of times it contains the word *behavior*. When our primary focus is on discrete behaviors, we end up ignoring the whole child.

That doesn't mean exemplary educators who avoid time outs, detentions, and other punishments are simply ignoring misbehavior. The real alternative to making children suffer for their offenses (or dangling goodies in front of them for doing what they're told) is to work *with* them to solve problems. A "working with" approach[13] asks more of the teacher than does a "doing to" approach, but it's a good deal more effective because even if the latter succeeds in imposing order temporarily, it does so by undermining students' moral development, compromising the relationship between teacher and students, and making it more difficult to establish a supportive environment for learning. In sum, giving the impression that we value children only when they're good doesn't promote goodness any more than giving the impression that we value children only when they succeed promotes success.

In an illuminating passage from her recent book *Learning to Trust,* Marilyn Watson explained that a teacher can make it clear to students that certain actions are unacceptable while still providing "a very deep kind of reassurance—the reassurance that she still care[s] about them and [is] not going to punish or desert them, even [if they do] something very bad." This posture allows "their best motives to surface," thus giving "space and support for them to reflect and to autonomously engage in the moral act of restitution"—that is, to figure out how to make things right after doing something wrong. "If we want our students to trust that we care for them," she concludes, "then we need to display our affection without demanding that they behave or perform in certain ways in return. It's not that we don't want and expect certain behaviors; we do. But our concern or affection does not depend on it."[14]

This is the heart of unconditional teaching, and Watson points out that it's easier to maintain this stance, even with kids who are frequently insulting or aggressive, if we keep in mind *why* they're acting that way. The idea is for the teacher to think about what these students need (emotionally speaking) and probably haven't received. That way, she can see "the vulnerable child behind the bothersome or menacing exterior."

The popular view is that children who misbehave are just "testing limits"—a phrase often used as a justification for imposing more limits, or punishments. But perhaps such children are testing something else entirely: the unconditionality of our care for them. Perhaps they're acting in unacceptable ways to see if we'll stop accepting them.

Thus, one teacher dealt with a particularly challenging child by sitting down with him and saying, "You know what[?] I really, really like you. You can keep doing all this stuff and it's not going to change my mind. It seems to me that you are trying to get me to dislike you, but it's not going to work. I'm not ever going to do that." This teacher added: "It was soon after that, and I'm not saying immediately, that his disruptive behaviors started to decrease."[15] The moral here is that unconditional acceptance is not only something all children deserve; it's also a powerfully effective way to help them become better people. It's more useful, practically speaking, than any "behavior management" plan could ever be.

Providing Unconditional Acceptance

Teaching in this way is not just a matter of how we respond to children after they do something wrong, of course. It's about the countless gestures that let them know we're glad to see them, that we trust and respect them, that we care what happens to them. It's about the real (and unconditional) respect we show by asking all students what *they* think about how things are going, and how we might do things differently, not the selective reinforcement we offer to some students when they please us.

Unconditional teachers are not afraid to be themselves with students—to act like real human beings rather than crisply controlling authority figures. Their classrooms have an appealing informality about them. They may bring in occasional treats for their students— *all* their students—for no particular reason. They may write notes to children, have lunch with them, respond from the heart to their journal entries. Such teachers listen carefully to what kids say and remember details about their lives: "Hey, Joanie. You said on Friday that your Mom might take you to the fair over the weekend. Did you go? Was it fun?"

It's not possible to like all one's students equally well, but unconditional teachers try hard not to play favorites. More than that, they do their best to find something appealing about each child and respond accordingly. They make it clear that, while there are certain expectations in the classroom—expectations that, ideally, the students themselves have helped to suggest—the teacher's basic affection need not be earned. Caring that has to be earned isn't real caring at all.

Accepting students for who they are—as opposed to for what they do—is integrally related to the idea of teaching the whole child. That connection is worth highlighting because the phrase "whole child" is sometimes interpreted to mean "more than academics," which suggests a fragmented education. The point isn't just to meet a student's emotional needs with this activity, her physical needs with that activity, her social needs with something else, and so on. Rather, it is an integrated self to whom we respond. It is a whole person whom we value. And to do so in any way that matters is to accept children unconditionally, even (perhaps especially) when they screw up or fall short.

It isn't easy to create these sorts of relationships when there's no time to know each student. Huge classes, huge schools, and short periods are impediments to more than academic achievement. That's why, once again, unconditional teachers understand the need to work for systemic change—for example, pressing for the demise of the factory-like American high school model, an impediment to good teaching if ever there was one. But in the meantime, within whatever structures we work, we need to think about whether our posture toward students really provides them with as much of the unconditional acceptance they need as possible.

Imagine that your students are invited to respond to a questionnaire several years after leaving the school. They're asked to indicate whether they agree or disagree—and how strongly—with statements such as: "Even when I wasn't proud of how I acted, even when I didn't do the homework, even when I got low test scores or didn't seem interested in what was being taught, I knew that [insert your name here] still cared about me."

How would you like your students to answer that sort of question? How do you think they will answer it?

Notes

1. Robert F. Hogan, "Foreword," in *Measuring Growth in English*, Paul B. Diederich (Urbana, IL: National Council of Teachers of English, 1974), p. iii.

2. Jodi Wilgoren, "Florida's Vouchers a Spur to Two Schools Left Behind," *New York Times*, March 14, 2000, pp. A1, A18.

3. See, for example, Edward L. Deci and Richard M. Ryan, "Human Autonomy: The Basis for True Self-Esteem," in *Efficacy, Agency, and Self-Esteem*, ed. Michael H. Kernis (New York: Plenum, 1995); and Michael H. Kernis, "Toward a Conceptualization of Optimal Self-Esteem," *Psychological Inquiry* 14, no. 1 (2003): 1–26.

4. John M. Chamberlain and David A. F. Haaga, "Unconditional Self-Acceptance and Psychological Health," *Journal of Rational-Emotive and Cognitive-Behavior Therapy* 19, no. 3 (Fall 2001): 163–76.

5. Carl R. Rogers, "A Theory of Therapy, Personality, and Interpersonal Relationships, as Developed in the Client-Centered Framework," in *Psychology: A Study of a Science, Study I: Conceptual and Systematic*, vol. 3, ed. Sigmund Koch (New York: McGraw-Hill, 1959).

6. Susan Harter, *The Construction of the Self: A Developmental Perspective* (New York: Guilford, 1999). Also, see Avi Assor, Guy Roth, and Edward L. Deci, "The Emotional Costs of Parents' Conditional Regard: A Self-Determination Theory Analysis," *Journal of Personality* 72, no. 1 (February 2004): 47–89.

7. Susan Harter, Donna B. Marold, Nancy R. Whitesell, and Gabrielle Cobbs, "A Model of the Effects of Perceived Parent and Peer Support on Adolescent False Self Behavior," *Child Development* 67, no. 2 (April 1996): 360–74.

8. Alfie Kohn, *Unconditional Parenting: Moving from Rewards and Punishments to Love and Reason* (New York: Atria Books, 2005).

9. Evi Makri-Botsari, "Causal Links between Academic Intrinsic Motivation, Self-Esteem, and Unconditional Acceptance by Teachers in High School Students," in *International Perspectives on Individual Differences*, vol. 2: *Self Perception*, eds. Richard J. Riding and Stephen G. Rayner (Westport, CT: Ablex, 2001).

10. Alfie Kohn, *Punished by Rewards: The Trouble with Gold Stars, Incentive Plans, A's, Praise, and Other Bribes* (Boston: Houghton Mifflin, 1993).

11. Nel Noddings, *The Challenge to Care in Schools: An Alternative Approach to Education* (New York: Teachers College Press, 1992).

12. Adele Faber and Elaine Mazlish, *How to Talk So Kids Can Learn* (New York: Rawson, 1995).

13. Child Development Project, *Ways We Want Our Class to Be: Class Meetings That Build Commitment to Kindness and Learning* (Oakland, CA: Developmental Studies Center, 1996); Rheta DeVries and Betty Zan, *Moral Classrooms, Moral Children: Creating a Constructivist Atmosphere in Early Education* (New York: Teachers College Press, 1994); and Alfie Kohn, *Beyond Discipline: From Compliance to Community* (Alexandria, VA: Association for Supervision and Curriculum Development, 1996).

14. Marilyn Watson, *Learning to Trust: Transforming Difficult Elementary Classrooms Through Developmental Discipline* (San Francisco: Jossey-Bass, 2003).

15. Ibid.

10.   Safety from the Inside Out

For many people, the idea of safety in an educational context brings to mind the problem of school violence, and specifically the string of shootings at schools across the country in recent years. Let's begin, then, by noting that the coverage of these events has obscured several important facts:

• The real horror is *that* young people die, not *where* they die. To be sure, there's something deeply unsettling about the juxtaposition of the words "violence" and "schools." But keep in mind that the vast majority of young homicide victims are killed at home, on the streets, or somewhere else other than school. During one three-year period in the 1990s, for example, about eighty homicides took place on school grounds . . . while more than eight *thousand* children were killed elsewhere. This is important to keep in mind both so that we recognize the full extent of the problem and so we don't exaggerate how dangerous schools really are.

• There is a tendency, upon hearing about stunning cases of school violence, to infer that adolescents are Public Enemy No. 1. But Mike Males, a sociologist, urges us to focus our attention on the "far more common phenomenon of adults killing kids." He points out that Americans blame teenagers too easily, and usually inaccurately, for what's wrong with our society.[1]

• When school violence does occur, low-income students of color are disproportionately likely to be the victims, notwithstanding Columbine and other notorious school-shooting incidents. If that fact is surprising, it may be because of the media's tacit assumption that any problem—crime, drugs, violence—is more newsworthy when white people in the suburbs are affected.

Yet another series of mistaken assumptions comes into play when educators and policy makers try to respond to violence—or to their fear of it. Questionable beliefs often lead to wrongheaded policies.

First, we Americans love to imagine that technical fixes will take care of complicated problems. (Remember the V-chip, which was supposed to be the solution to children's exposure to violent television programming?) Some people still cling to the hope that schools can be made safer if we just install enough surveillance cameras and metal detectors. In reality, though, it's simply not feasible to guard every doorway or monitor every screen. The number of cameras at one Washington, D.C., high school was recently doubled, from thirty-two to sixty-four, but the principal admitted that it's hard to keep guns "on the outside of the school unless we become armed camps, and I don't think anyone wants to send their child to an armed camp." His comments were reported in a newspaper article that was aptly headlined "Trust, Not Cameras, Called Best Prevention."[2]

Pedro Noguera, who teaches at New York University, put it this way: "Design and staffing of schools are driven by security concerns, but no thought is given to how these designs and atmospheres make students and [teachers] feel. If we use prisons as our models for safe schools—well, prisons are not safe places, right? Safety comes from human relations. I'd say we'd do much better to invest in counselors than armed guards."[3]

Second, when we do focus on the human element of violence prevention, we often assume that students just need to be taught the appropriate skills.[4] This model is so simple and familiar to us that we don't even think of it as a model at all. It seems a matter of common sense that if children don't pay attention to what someone else is saying, they would benefit from some remedial listening skills. If they fail to lend a hand to someone in distress, they need to hone their helping skills. If they're reluctant to stand up for themselves, they're candidates for assertiveness training. Thus, by analogy, if violence keeps breaking out, all we need to do is teach students the skills of conflict resolution.

Unfortunately, skills are not enough. Most kids already know how to listen, how to help, and how to assert themselves. The question is why they sometimes lack the *disposition* to act in these ways. It's much the same with efforts to raise academic achievement: A skills-based approach has its limits if we ignore the question of how interested students are in what they're being taught. Such efforts may even do more harm than good if an emphasis on teaching basic skills makes school downright unappealing. The same goes for literacy in particular: Consider how many children know how to read, but don't. In short, what matters is not only whether people can learn, or act, in a particular way, but whether they have the inclination to do so.

Why, then, do we spend so much time teaching skills? For one thing, this implies that it's the students who need fixing. If something more complicated than a lack of know-how is involved, we might have to question our own practices and premises, which can be uncomfortable. Moreover, a focus on skills allows us to ignore the structural elements of a classroom (or school or family). If students hurt one other, it's easier for us to try to deal with each individual's actions than it is to ask which elements of the system might have contributed to the problem.

A skills-based approach is also compatible with behaviorism, whose influence over our schools—and, indeed, over all of American society—is difficult to overstate. Behaviorism dismisses anything that can't be reduced to a discrete set of observable and measurable behaviors. This dogma lies behind segmented instructional techniques, as well as many of the most popular approaches to character education, classroom management, and our practices with students who have special needs.

When we're preoccupied with behaviors, we're less likely to dig deep in order to understand the reasons, values, and motives that give rise to those behaviors. We end up embracing superficial responses, such as trying to improve the climate of a school by forcing students to dress alike. (Among other limitations of a policy like this, our assumption seems to be that we can reduce aggression by borrowing an idea from the military.) But any time we talk about changing students' "behaviors," we run the risk of ignoring the students who are doing the behaving. We lose the human beings behind the actions. Thus, we may come to see students as computers that can be reprogrammed, or pets that can be retrained, or empty receptacles that can be refilled—all dangerously misleading metaphors. We offer behavioral instruction in more appropriate ways to express anger, but the violence continues because we haven't gotten anywhere near where the problem is.

It often doesn't work very well, then, to employ technical fixes or to teach skills. But there's a third response that isn't merely ineffective; it's actively counterproductive. I have in mind the policies that follow from assuming we can stamp out violence—or create safety—by coercive means. In her book *The Peaceable School*, Vicky Dill remarked that while it can be bad to have no plan for dealing with school violence, "it can be much worse to have a simplistic, authoritarian policy."[5]

A reliance on old-fashioned discipline, with threats of punishments for offenders, not only distracts us from dealing with the real causes of aggression, but in effect *models* bullying and power for students. Many school officials fail to understand this fact and end up throwing fuel on the fire by responding to signs of student distress with ever-harsher measures. Consistent with the tendency to ignore the structural causes of problems, they seem to think sheer force will make the bad stuff go away; if students are made to suffer for doing something wrong, they will see the error of their ways. When that proves ineffective, it's assumed that *more* punishment—along with tighter regulations and less trust—will do the trick.[6]

The shootings at Columbine provoked a general panic in which hundreds of students across the country were arrested, while "countless others were suspended or expelled for words or deeds perceived as menacing."[7] The fear here is understandable: Administrators wondered whether their district, too, might be incubating killers. But we need to understand the difference between *overreaction,* such as closing down a school to search for bombs after a student makes an offhand joke, and *destructive reactions*, such as coercive policies.

A particularly egregious example of the latter is the so-called "zero tolerance" approach, which is based on the premise that harsh punishment will work better if it's meted out indiscriminately—indeed, in robotic fashion. It took a few years before this strategy began to attract critical attention in the media.[8] Research, meanwhile, has been accumulating to confirm that it makes no sense at all. One study discovered that students in schools with such a policy "actually report feeling less safe . . . than do students in schools with more moderate policies."[9] That subjective impression is supported by objective evidence: Another analysis showed that "even after schools with zero tolerance policies had implemented them for more than four years, those schools were still less safe than schools without such policies."[10] Moreover, zero tolerance doesn't affect everyone equally: African-American and Latino students are more likely than their white counterparts to be targeted by this sort of punitive discipline.[11] As a society, we seem to have a lot more tolerance for the misbehavior of white children.

The finding that schools become less safe as a result of adopting zero-tolerance policies will sound paradoxical only to those readers who believe that threats and punishment can create safety. In reality, safety is put at risk by such an approach. A safe school environment is one where students are able to really know and trust—and be known and trusted by—adults.[12] Those bonds, however, are ruptured by a system that's about doing things *to* students who act inappropriately rather than working *with* them to solve problems. "The first casualty" of zero-tolerance policies "is the central, critical relationship between teacher and student, a relationship that is now being damaged or broken in favor of tough-sounding, impersonal, uniform procedures."[13]

Zero tolerance is bad enough, but the situation becomes even worse when the punishments in question are so harsh that students are turned into criminals. Across the country, the *New York Times* reported in early 2004, "schools are increasingly sending students into the juvenile justice systems for the sort of adolescent misbehavior that used to be handled by school administrators."[14] Apart from the devastating effects that turning children over to the police can have on their lives, the school's climate is curdled because administrators send the message that a student who does something wrong may be taken away in handcuffs and, in effect, exiled from the community. Here we see the *reductio ad absurdum* of trying to improve schools by relying on threats and fear.

There are many explanations for this deeply disturbing trend, including the loss of school-based mental health services due to budget cuts. But Mark Soler of the Youth Law Center, a public interest group that protects at-risk children, observes that these days "zero tolerance is fed less by fear of crime and more by high-stakes testing. Principals want to get rid of kids they perceive as trouble" because doing so may have an advantageous effect on their school's overall test results.[15]

School safety is at risk, that is, not merely because some educators wrongly believe that stricter or more consistent application of punitive discipline will help, but because of the pressure to raise test scores. What's more, that same pressure, which leads some people to regard students in trouble as disposable commodities, also has the effect of squeezing out efforts to help them avoid getting into trouble in the first place. Programs to promote conflict resolution and to address bullying and other sorts of violence are being eliminated because educators are themselves being bullied into focusing on standardized test results to the exclusion of everything else. Scott Poland, a school psychologist and expert in crisis intervention, writes: "School principals have told me that they would like to devote curriculum time to topics such as managing anger, violence prevention and learning to get along with others regardless of race and ethnicity, but . . . [they are] under tremendous pressure to raise academic scores on the state accountability test."[16]

Thus, argues Margaret McKenna, the president of Lesley University, "Some of the most important lessons of Columbine have been all but forgotten—left behind, so to speak, in no small measure because of . . . the No Child Left Behind Act. The law's narrow focus on yearly improvement in test scores has [made schools] . . . even less conducive to teachers' knowing their students well." To drive home the point that our priorities have become skewed, she observes that "the test scores at Columbine High were among the highest in Colorado."[17]

Even in those cases where a student's actions pose a significant risk to the safety of others, the first question for an educator should not be, "Have we used sufficient force to stamp out this threat?" but "What have we done to address the underlying issues here? How can we transform our schools into places that meet students' needs so there is less chance that someone will be moved to lash out in fury?"

Here's a different way to look at it: We need to stop talking primarily about creating peaceful schools, which is not a particularly ambitious or meaningful goal. Schools, after all, are completely peaceful at 3 a.m. Similarly, a classroom full of docile, unquestioning students may be peaceful, even if they aren't learning much of value, don't care much about one another, and would rather be someplace else. What we need to work for is the creation of schools that are *peaceable*—that is, committed to the value of peace and to helping students feel safe, in all senses of that word.[18]

Physical safety, the most obvious kind, has understandably been the top priority, particularly where it seems to be in short supply. But intellectual and emotional safety matter, too—in their own rights and also because they're related to physical safety. Bullying and other violent acts are less likely to happen in a school that feels like a caring community, a place where children experience a sense of connection to one another and to adults, a place where they come to think in the plural and feel a sense of belonging. That's the polar opposite of a school where kids are picked on for being different or uncool, to the point that they fear entering certain hallways or sections of the cafeteria. Caring school communities don't let that happen: They regard any evidence of nasty cliques or hurtful exclusion as serious problems to be addressed. They do everything possible so that no one fears being laughed at, picked on, or humiliated.

These efforts take place in individual classrooms and also as a matter of school policy. Proactive efforts to build community and resolve conflicts are important, but so too must educators focus on what gets in the way of safety and community. Thus, teachers not only hold class meetings on a regular basis so that students can participate in making decisions; they also use these meetings to address troubling things that may be going on. One teacher spoke up after a math lesson, for example, to talk with her students about

> something I *don't* like and I *don't* want to hear because it makes me feel bad, and if it makes me feel bad it probably makes someone else in here feel bad. It's these two words. (She writes "That's easy" on the chalkboard and draws a circle around the phrase.). . . . When I am struggling and trying so hard, [hearing that phrase] makes me feel kind of dumb or stupid. Because I am thinking, gosh, if it's so easy why am I having so much trouble with it? . . . And what's one of our rules in here? It's to be considerate of others and their feelings.[19]

Such an intervention may be motivated not only by a general commitment to making sure that students don't feel bad, but also by a desire to promote high-quality learning. There are intellectual costs when students don't feel safe to take risks. A classroom where kids worry if their questions will be thought silly is a classroom where unselfconscious engagement with ideas is less likely to take place. (Of course, students often are unwilling to ask questions or acknowledge that they're struggling for fear of the reaction from the teacher, not just from their classmates.)

On a schoolwide level, intellectual and emotional safety require that students are freed from being rated and ranked, freed from the public pressure to show how smart they are—or, even worse, how much smarter they are than everyone else. Awards assemblies and honor rolls are very effective ways to destroy the sense of safety that supports a willingness to learn. Some schools that pride themselves on their commitment to high standards and achievement have created a climate that really isn't about learning at all—let alone about caring. Such places are more about results than about kids. Their students often feel as though they're in a pressure cooker, where some must fail in order that others can succeed. The message students get is that other people are potential obstacles to their own success.[20]

There is much more to be said, of course, about how and why to build community, to meet kids' needs, to create a culture of safety and caring.[21] The benefits of doing so are most pronounced in schools that have more low-income students,[22] yet such schools are often distinguished instead by punitive discipline and a climate of control. However, schools in affluent areas may also feel unsafe in various ways. Columbine High School was reportedly a place where bullying was common and a sharply stratified social structure was allowed to flourish, one in which athletes were deified. (Some of these sports stars taunted other students mercilessly "while school authorities looked the other way."[23]) In some suburban schools, the curriculum is chock-full of rigorous Advanced Placement courses and the parking lot glitters with pricey SUVs, but one doesn't have to look hard to find students who are starving themselves, cutting themselves, or medicating themselves, as well as students who are taking out their frustrations on those who sit lower on the social food chain.

Even in a school free of weapons, children may feel unsafe and unhappy. And that's reason enough to rethink our assumptions, redesign our policies, and redouble our commitment to creating a different kind of educational culture.

Notes

1. Mike Males, "Who's Really Killing Our Schoolkids?" *Los Angeles Times,* May 31, 1999. Also see other writings by Males, including his book *The Scapegoat Generation: America's War on Adolescents* (Monroe, ME: Common Courage Press, 1996).

2. The article, by Debbi Wilgoren, appeared in the *Washington Post* on February 3, 2004, p. A-7.

3. Pedro A. Noguera, "School Safety Lessons Learned: Urban Districts Report Progress," *Education Week,* May 30, 2001, p. 15.

4. This section is adapted from my article "The Limits of Teaching Skills," *Reaching Today's Youth,* Summer 1997, pp. 15–16.

5. Vicky Schreiber Dill, *A Peaceable School: Creating a Culture of Non-Violence* (Bloomington, IN: Phi Delta Kappa, 1997), p. 24. Also see *Dangerous Schools,* Irwin A. Hyman and Pamela A. Snook (San Francisco: Jossey-Bass, 1999), an excerpt from which appeared in the March 2000 issue of *Phi Delta Kappan.*

6. This section is adapted from my article "Constant Frustration and Occasional Violence: The Legacy of American High Schools," *American School Board Journal,* September 1999. For more on the counterproductive effects of—and some alternatives to—punitive "consequences" and rewards, see my book *Beyond Discipline: From Compliance to Community* (Alexandria, VA: Association for Supervision and Curriculum Development, 1996).

7. Caroline Hendrie, "In Schools, A Sigh of Relief as Tense Spring Draws to a Close," *Education Week,* June 23, 1999.

8. For example, see Dirk Johnson, "Schools' New Watchword: Zero Tolerance," *New York Times,* December 1, 1999; Jesse Katz, "Taking Zero Tolerance to the Limit," *Los Angeles Times,* March 1, 1998.

9. This quotation is from Robert Blum of the University of Minnesota. The study, to which he contributed, was published in the *Journal of School Health* and summarized in Darcia Harris Bowman, "School 'Connectedness' Makes for Healthier Students, Study Suggests," *Education Week,* April 24, 2002, p. 16.

10. John H. Holloway, "The Dilemma of Zero Tolerance," *Educational Leadership,* December 2001/January 2002, p. 84. The analysis summarized here was published by the National Center for Education Statistics in 1998. Also, for an excellent review of the effects of such policies, see Russ Skiba and Reece Peterson, "The Dark Side of Zero Tolerance: Can Punishment Lead to Safe Schools?" *Phi Delta Kappan,* January 1999, pp. 372–76, 381–82.

11. A report by a civil rights group called The Advancement Project, based on an analysis of federal statistics, was described in Kenneth J. Cooper, "Group Finds Racial Disparity in Schools' 'Zero Tolerance,'" *Washington Post,* June 15, 2000.

12. For example, see *In Schools We Trust,* Deborah Meier (Boston: Beacon, 2002).

13. William Ayers and Bernardine Dohrn, "Have We Gone Overboard with Zero Tolerance?" *Chicago Tribune,* November 21, 1999.

14. Sara Rimer, "Unruly Students Facing Arrest, Not Detention," *New York Times,* January 4, 2004, p. A-1.

15. That explanation also makes sense to Augustina Reyes of the University of Houston: "If teachers are told, 'Your [test] scores go down, you lose your job,' all of a sudden your values shift very quickly. Teachers think, 'With bad kids in my class, I'll have lower achievement on my tests, so I'll use discretion and remove that kid.'" Both Reyes and Soler are quoted in Annette Fuentes, "Discipline and Punish," *Nation,* December 15, 2003, pp. 17–20.

16. "The Non-Hardware Side of School Safety," *NASP* [National Association of School Psychologists] *Communique* 28, no. 6 (March 2000). Poland made the same point while testifying at a congressional hearing on school violence in March 1999—a month before the shootings at Columbine.

17. Margaret A. McKenna, "Lessons Left Behind," *Washington Post,* April 20, 2004, p. A-19.

18. The distinction between peaceful and peaceable was popularized by Bill Kreidler, who worked with Educators for Social Responsibility and wrote several books about conflict resolution. He died in 2000 at the unripe age of forty-eight.

19. Paul Cobb, Erna Yackel, and Terry Wood, "Young Children's Emotional Acts While Engaged in Mathematical Problem Solving," in *Affect and Mathematical Problem Solving: A New Perspective,* eds. Douglas B. McLeod and Verna M. Adams (New York: Springer-Verlag, 1989), pp. 130–31.

20. Our culture's uncritical acceptance of the ideology of competition is such that even people who acknowledge the damaging effects of an "excessive" emphasis on winning may continue to assert that competition, per se, is inevitable or productive. If this assertion is typically unaccompanied by evidence, that's probably because the available data support exactly the opposite position—namely, that a win/lose arrangement tends to hold us back from doing our best work and from optimal learning. I've reviewed some of that evidence in *No Contest: The Case Against Competition* (Boston: Houghton Mifflin, 1986).

21. See my article "Caring Kids: The Role of the Schools," *Phi Delta Kappan,* March 1991, pp. 496–506 (available at www.alfiekohn.org/teaching/cktrots .htm); and chapter 7 ("The Classroom as Community") of *Beyond Discipline.* Many other writers, of course, have also addressed this question.

22. Victor Battistich, Daniel Solomon, Dong-il Kim, Marilyn Watson, and Eric Schaps, "Schools as Communities, Poverty Levels of Student Populations, and Students' Attitudes, Motives, and Performance: A Multilevel Analysis," *American Educational Research Journal* 32 (1995): 627–58.

23. Lorraine Adams and Dale Russakoff, "Dissecting Columbine's Cult of the Athlete," *Washington Post,* June 12, 1999, p. A-1.

11. Bad Signs

You can tell quite a lot about what goes on in a classroom or a school even if you visit after everyone has gone home. Just by looking at the walls—or, more precisely, what's on the walls—it's possible to get a feel for the educational priorities, the attitudes about children, even the assumptions about human nature of the people in charge.

A chart that I created more than a decade ago called "What to Look For in a Classroom" listed some "Good Signs" along with "Possible Reasons to Worry."[1] Among the latter: walls that are mostly bare, giving the building a stark, institutional feel; and posted displays that suggest either a focus on control (lists of rules or, even worse, punishments) or an emphasis on relative performance (charts that include grades or other evaluations of each student).

Because I've done so elsewhere, I won't take time here to explain why such lists and charts make me shudder. Instead, I'd like to consider a few signs and posters that are generally regarded as innocuous or even inspiring. Particularly deserving of a closer look are two specific posters as well as a broader category that includes a seemingly unlimited number of examples.

"NO WHINING": This sign—which sometimes consists of the word "whining" with a diagonal red slash through it—is meant to send a message to students, and that message seems to be: "I don't want to hear your complaints about anything that you're being made to do (or prevented from doing)." To be sure, this is not an unusual sentiment; in fact, it may be exactly what your boss would like to say to you. But that doesn't mean it's admirable to insist, perhaps with a bit of a smirk, that students should just do whatever they're told, regardless of whether it's reasonable or how it makes them feel. If *we* might respond with frustration or resentment to receiving such a message, why would we treat students that way? "No whining" mostly underscores the fact that the person saying this has more power than the people to whom it's said.

 Originally published in *Kappa Delta Pi Record*, Fall 2010

Of course, the sign could be read more literally: Perhaps it's just a certain style of complaining, a wheedling tone, that's being targeted. Frankly, I don't love that sound either, but should someone's tone of voice really take precedence over the content of whatever he or she is trying to say to us? I'm less annoyed by whining than I am by the disproportionate reaction to it on the part of adults. It's fine to offer an occasional, matter-of-fact reminder to a child that people tend to be put off by certain ways of asking for something, but our priority should be to make sure that kids know we're listening, that our relationship with them doesn't depend on the way they talk to us. Besides, young children in particular need to have some way of expressing their frustration. We don't let them hit, scream, or curse. Now we're insisting that they can't even use a tone of voice that's, well, insistent?

Regardless of how "whining" is defined, going to the trouble of posting a sign about it suggests that our own convenience is what matters most to us (since it's obviously easier for anyone in a position of authority if those being ordered to do something comply without question). It also implies that we're unwilling to reconsider our own actions and uninterested in having students question authority—despite the fact that education at its best consists of helping them to do precisely that.[2]

"ONLY POSITIVE ATTITUDES ALLOWED BEYOND THIS POINT": I've seen this poster on classroom doors in a public school in Minnesota, a Catholic school in Indiana, and a quasi-progressive Friends school in Massachusetts. Each time I came across it, I found myself imagining how its message might be reworded for satirical purposes. Once I came up with "Have a Nice Day . . . Or Else." Another time I fantasized about secretly removing the poster at night and replacing it with one that reads "My Mental Health Is So Precarious That All of You Had Better Pretend You're Happy."

I've long been convinced that dark stuff sometimes lurks just behind the huge, brittle smiles and the voices that swoop into unnaturally high registers in front of little children. Even apart from the treacly style in which it's often delivered, the compulsive tendency to praise kids when they do something helpful may reflect the pessimistic assumption that the action was a fluke: Children must be marinated in "Good job!"s whenever they happen to do something nice; otherwise they'd never act that way again.[3] The more compulsive (and squeaky) the use of positive reinforcement, the bleaker the underlying view of children—or maybe of our species.

But back to the sign. Putting students on notice that their attitudes had better damn well be positive tells us less about what makes for an optimal learning environment than it does about the needs (if not neediness) of the person who sends this message. Kids don't require a classroom that's relentlessly upbeat; they require a place where they'll feel safe to express whatever they're feeling, even if at the moment that happens to be sad or angry or scared. They need a place, in other words, where negativity is allowed. Bad feelings don't vanish in an environment of mandatory cheer—they just get swept under the rug where people end up tripping over them, so to speak.[4] What you or I may describe as a negative *attitude,* meanwhile, may be an entirely appropriate response to an unfair rule, an intimidating climate, or a task that seems pointless or impossible. To exclude such responses from students is to refuse to think seriously about what may have given rise to their negativity (see "No Whining," above).

INSPIRATIONAL POSTERS: Far more common than any specific message, including the two I've mentioned here, is a whole class of posters that might be described as "inspirational." Taped up in elementary, middle, and high schools across the country—outside the main office, in the cafeteria and the library, on individual classroom walls—we find these earnest, interchangeable calls to greatness, typically superimposed on gorgeous fading photographs. "You can if you think you can!" "Reach for the stars!" "Achievement is within your grasp!" "Winners make the effort!" "This year I choose success!" And on and on.

At this point I should probably confess that I don't much care for posters on school walls, period. It may seem like a harmless way to cover up painted cement blocks, but there's something impersonal and generic about items that weren't created by, or even for, the particular individuals who spend time in this building. Show me a school that adorns its walls with posters created by distant corporations, and I'll show you a school where it's possible the same could be said of its curriculum.

But if commercial posters in general don't gladden the heart of a visitor, there's something uniquely off-putting about *these* posters, which show up in all sorts of workplaces, not just schools. And it seems I'm not alone in this reaction, judging by the popularity of a series of parodies marketed under the name "Demotivators." One of these posters features a dramatic image of the pyramids along with the caption: "ACHIEVEMENT—You can do anything you set your mind to when you have vision, determination, and an endless supply of expendable labor." Another depicts a packet of fast-food French fries; it says: "POTENTIAL—Not everyone gets to be an astronaut when they grow up." On a third poster, a leaping salmon is about to wind up in the jaws of a bear: "AMBITION—The journey of a thousand miles sometimes ends very, very badly."[5]

Let's not just satirize, though; let's analyze. The exhortatory slogans found on motivational posters, like those in motivational speeches and books, tend to offer a combination of strenuous uplift and an emphasis on self-sufficiency. They tell us that, individually, we can do anything if we just set our minds to it. The trouble with this sort of encouragement becomes clearer when we begin to think about some of the specific things that students may conclude they can do.

Here's the first problem: The assurance that you can achieve anything you desire through hard work stretches the truth beyond recognition. And it's in the neighborhoods where children are most likely to hear about the wondrous results that await anyone with perseverance and a dream that the claim is hardest to defend.

"You can be the valedictorian!" With certain goals, the news is even worse. It's not just that being the valedictorian is an unrealistic expectation for most students; it's that this status, like so much else in our schools and our society, is set up as a zero-sum game. If I become the valedictorian, then you can't—and vice versa. In a

competitive environment, our dreams are mutually exclusive. This fact the posters somehow neglect to mention.

"You can get into Harvard!" And what happens when I, like 93 percent of the other self-selected and mostly superqualified applicants, receive my rejection letter from Cambridge? What if I chose success and reached for the stars and stayed true to my goals—only to wind up with nothing? Some students will become angry, concluding, not unreasonably, that they have been lied to. But others will blame themselves. And that's problem number two: "The flip side of positivity is thus a harsh insistence on personal responsibility," as Barbara Ehrenreich observed in her recent book *Bright-Sided: How the Relentless Promotion of Positive Thinking Has Undermined America.* If you fail, "it must [be] because you didn't try hard enough, didn't believe firmly enough in the inevitability of your success."[6]

And who benefits when the have-nots are led to think that way? Suffice it to say that nothing maintains the current arrangement of power more effectively than an approach that ignores the current arrangement of power. Rather than being invited to consider the existence of structural barriers and pronounced disparities in resources and opportunities, we're fed the line that there are no limits to what each of us can accomplish on our own if we just buckle down.

Notice, too, that inspirational posters are almost always generic, the implication being that "success" or "achievement," per se, is desirable; it doesn't matter what exactly one wants to achieve or at what one is trying to succeed. Any dream will do. But is that a conviction we're really prepared to endorse? And again, as they say in Latin, *cui bono?* Whose interests are served when we look at things that way?

"You can get an A!" For example, what if success is defined in terms of high grades, as is the case in traditional schools? The available research suggests that there are three predictable effects when students are led to focus on bringing home better report cards: They tend to become less interested in the learning itself, to think in a more superficial fashion, and to prefer the easiest possible task. But who is going to bother rethinking the value of rating students with letters or numbers—or on the specific tasks involved, like memoriz-

ing facts for a test or filling out worksheets, that determine who gets which grades—if the goal is just "success," and that's equated with getting an A? Do we want to send the message that this objective is equivalent to coming up with a novel solution to a meaningful intellectual challenge? Or that making a million dollars is just as worthy as working for a more just society?[7]

When motivational posters fail to make the relevant distinctions among dreams (or kinds of "achievement"), when we fail to encourage critical thought about these issues, the dominant goals and values of our culture are accepted by default. Is hard work *always* a good thing? Who gets to decide on the nature and purpose of that work? These are precisely the kinds of questions you're less inclined to ask if you've been told "Your attitude determines your future." The message of the self-help movement has always been: Adjust yourself to conditions as you find them because those conditions are immutable; all you can do is decide on the spirit in which to approach them (hint: we recommend a can-do spirit). To do well is to fit in, and to fit in is to perpetuate the structures into which you are being fit.

Am I being too hard on, or expecting too much from, a simple poster? Well, precisely because they're so pervasive—and accepted so uncritically—I think it's worth digging into the hidden premises of their chirpy banalities. Just because something is generally regarded as uncontroversial doesn't mean it's value-neutral. Imagine if a very different sort of poster appeared in your local high school—one that said, for example: "Some children are born into poverty; others are born with trust funds"—and picture what the accompanying illustration might look like. Or suppose we put up a sign that featured this remark by the late George Carlin: "It's called the American dream because you have to be asleep to believe in it." Undoubtedly some people would complain that these sentiments were too controversial. But where is the outrage over the subliminal values of a poster that airily assures us, "The sky's the limit!"?

One measure of the ideological uses to which inspirational slogans are put is the fact that they seem to be employed with particular intensity in the schools of low-income children of color. Here the self-empowerment agenda serves as more than background decor, and Jonathan Kozol has incisively pointed out the political implications of making African American students chant, "Yes, I can! I know I can!" or "If it is to be, it's up to me." Such slogans are very popular with conservative white people, he notes, because "if it's up to 'them,' the message seems to be, it isn't up to 'us,' which appears to sweep the deck of many pressing and potentially disruptive and expensive obligations we may otherwise believe our nation needs to contemplate." He adds: "Auto-hypnotic slogans" such as "I'm smart! I know that I'm smart" are rarely heard in suburban schools where "the potential of most children is assumed."[8]

I'd love to see a research study that counted the number of motivational posters (along with other self-help, positive-thinking materials and activities) in a school and then assessed certain other features of that school. My hypothesis: The popularity of inspirational slogans will be correlated with a lower probability that students are invited to play a meaningful role in decision-making, as well as less evidence of an emphasis on critical thinking threaded through the curriculum and a less welcoming attitude toward questioning authority. I'd also predict that the schools decorated with these posters are more likely to be run by administrators who brag about the school's success by conventional indicators and are less inclined to call those criteria into question or challenge troubling mandates handed down from above (such as zero-tolerance discipline policies or pressures to raise test scores).

Good Signs

It would seem unsporting, and perhaps unduly negative, to conclude this little essay without suggesting what might replace all of those mass-produced exhortations to stop whining, remain (or pretend to be) upbeat, and remember to triumph over adversity. Perhaps we can begin with phrases that seem suitable for posting to someone with a more progressive sensibility. All else being close to equal, I'd be thrilled to send my children to a school whose walls featured variations on the timeless reminder to "Question authority." And imagine if the principal's office contained a framed printout of this reminder from researcher Linda McNeil: "Measurable outcomes may be the least significant results of learning." Visitors would be reassured that such an administrator understood a lot more about education than do most politicians.

Similarly, what could be more refreshing than the large sign tacked up in a Washington state classroom that said "Think for yourself; the teacher might be wrong"? Or, for those who prefer a more ironic tone, consider this commentary on control (of children by adults, or of educators by policy makers) that I spotted in an Idaho classroom: "The beatings will continue until morale improves."

I'd also be happy to wander the halls of a middle school where every student has a sign on his or her locker that says "[Name of student] is currently reading . . . " accompanied by a photocopy of the cover of the book in question.[9] Beyond the specific information being conveyed, compare the cumulative impact of hundreds of such announcements with those well-meaning but insipid reminders ("Read!") that appear in libraries. In fact, I like to see school walls filled with all sorts of information about, and personal mementos of, the people who spend their days there. (And that includes the adults: When Deborah Meier was its principal, the central corridor of the Mission Hill School in Boston had a large bulletin board filled with childhood photos of the school's teachers.)

When I visit traditional classrooms, grimacing at so much of what's on the walls, I find myself wondering why they're not filled with stuff done by the students. The answer to that question, unfortunately, may be that the students haven't been allowed to do much that's worth displaying. Hence my original hypothesis, that the room decor may speak volumes about the theory and practice of instruction. I once spent time in a Long Island elementary school classroom where elaborate animal habitats were being created, and students had posted lists of "problems we faced when designing and constructing" these habitats. The displays gave evidence of complex thought, perseverance in overcoming those problems, classwide cooperation—and the fact that the teacher's priority was to help these kids learn to think like scientists rather than just memorizing scientific facts for a test.

The broader moral is that the best classrooms, regardless of age level or academic discipline, often feature signs, exhibits, or other materials obviously created by the students themselves. And that includes students' ideas for how to create a sense of community and learn together most effectively—as opposed to a list of rules imposed by the teacher (or summarized on a commercial poster).

In fact, we're ultimately led to ask a meta-question: not just "What should go on the walls?" but "Who decides what goes on the walls?" I'd be willing to bet that just about all of the signs and posters about which I've been raising concerns here were put up by the adults without even consulting the students. (What kid would suggest "No Whining"?) In fact, the exclusion of the people we're there to teach may be the most significant, though invisible, implication of what usually goes on the walls. To reverse this, we'd need not only to rethink what we're posting but whether the school in which these items are displayed is one that invites students to participate in thinking about what they do as well as the look of the place where they do it.

Notes

1. The revised version of this chart appears as Appendix B of *The Schools Our Children Deserve: Moving Beyond Traditional Classrooms and "Tougher Standards"* (Boston: Houghton Mifflin, 1999) and at www.alfiekohn.org/teaching/wtlfiacchart.htm.

2. For example, see my article "Challenging Students—And How to Have More of Them," which appears as chapter 2 of this volume.

3. For more on this topic, see my article "Five Reasons to Stop Saying 'Good Job!'" *Young Children,* September 2001, pp. 24–28 (available at www.alfiekohn.org/parenting/gj.htm).

4. Deborah Meier once commented that if a child claims one of her classmates doesn't like her, "We need to resist reassuring her that it's not true and getting the classmate to confirm it; then we must ask ourselves what has led to this idea. Probably there is truth to the cry for help, and our refusal to admit it may simply lead the child to hide her hurt more deeply. Do we do too

much reassuring—'It doesn't hurt,' 'It'll be okay'—and not enough exploring, joining with the child's queries, fears, thoughts?" ("For Safety's Sake,"
Educational Horizons 83, no. 1 [2004]: 59).

5. For more, see www.despair.com/viewall.html.
6. Barbara Ehrenreich, *Bright-Sided: How the Relentless Promotion of Positive Thinking Has Undermined America* (New York: Metropolitan Books, 2009), p. 8.
7. On the effects of grades, see my books *The Schools Our Children Deserve* and *Punished by Rewards: The Trouble with Gold Stars, Incentive Plans, A's, Praise, and Other Bribes* (Boston: Houghton Mifflin, 1993). On the poorer psychological and social outcomes for people for whom being rich (or famous or attractive) is a priority, see *The High Price of Materialism*, Tim Kasser (Cambridge, MA: MIT Press, 2003). I summarized some of the research described in that book in an article called "In Pursuit of Affluence, at a High Price," *New York Times,* February 2, 1999, available online at www.alfiekohn.org/managing/ipoa.htm.
8. Jonathan Kozol, *The Shame of the Nation: The Restoration of Apartheid Schooling in America* (New York: Crown, 2005), pp. 35–36.
9. See www.choiceliteracy.com/public/1062.cfm. I learned of these signs from Susan Ohanian's Web site.

Four: The Big Picture

Education Policy

12.   Feel-Bad Education: The Cult of Rigor and the Loss of Joy

"Why are our schools not places of joy?" This question, posed by John Goodlad exactly twenty years ago, was both a summary of his landmark study of American classrooms and a plea for his readers to realize that a place called school didn't have to be as bleak as it was.

Today things are different, of course. Today we rarely even ask the question.

That so few children seem to take pleasure from what they're doing on a given weekday morning, that the default emotional state in classrooms seems to alternate between anxiety and boredom, doesn't even alarm us. Worse: Happiness in schools is something for which educators may feel obliged to apologize when it does make an appearance. After all, they wouldn't want to be accused of offering a "feel-good" education.

Not much chance of that, though. Children these days are likely to be on the receiving end of a curriculum specified by powerful and distant others. Those in poor neighborhoods can count on having to sit through prefabricated lessons, often minutely scripted, whose purpose is not to promote thinking, much less the joy of discovery, but to raise test scores.

Students tend to be regarded not as subjects but as objects, not as learners but as workers. By repeating words like "accountability" and "results" often enough, the people who devise and impose this approach to schooling evidently succeed in rationalizing what amounts to a policy of feel-bad education.

Countless adolescents, meanwhile, face the prospect of a dishonorable discharge from high school purely on the basis of their performance on a state test. Those of their peers who are more successful at the rating-and-ranking game don't worry about diplomas. Rather, they are under pressure to attain stellar scores on a different exam while maintaining impossibly high grades and a collection of impressive extracurricular activities. The objective is to assure their admission to the sort of college to which no one's admission is, in fact, assured.

Even in the absence of active misery, the mood in many schools calls to mind Thoreau's famous phrase: quiet desperation. Students count off the hours remaining until dismissal, the days until the weekend, the weeks until vacation. It is the common experience of tots and teenagers, strugglers and achievers.

This situation isn't entirely new, of course. Joy has been in short supply in some classrooms for as long as there have *been* classrooms. But I join Deborah Meier in wondering whether things are worse now, not only because more people are less happy but because this is taken for granted; we don't even see it as a problem that requires our attention.

To be sure, it's theoretically possible to get carried away in the opposite direction. One could adopt a philosophy of hedonism that emphasizes pleasure to the exclusion of all other goods. One could even set up a classroom in which students are always having a good time but rarely learning anything of value. But neither that philosophy nor that practice was particularly common even during the storied 1960s; today, both are vanishingly rare, beholden as we are to a cult of rigor.

It's simply stunning, therefore, that some traditionalists actually complain about an excessive concern with children's happiness. Earlier this year, I came across an essay by an administrator who attempted to explain the supposed inferiority of U.S. schools by asserting that, whereas parents in other countries ask their children, "What did you learn in school today?" American parents ask, "Did you enjoy school today?"

Would that it were true! The author Frank McCourt, who taught at a prestigious New York City high school for eighteen years, told the journalist John Merrow that only once in all that time had a parent ever asked him, "Is my child enjoying school?" Instead, all he—and, presumably, the students themselves—heard from parents were questions about test scores, college applications, and getting the work done.

It's one thing to try to justify a state of enforced joylessness. But how is it possible to deny the reality, to turn things inside out and claim that we're *too* concerned with wanting children to be happy at school? Such a claim may be unjustifiable, but its style is not unfamiliar. It's one more example of how a distorted description of educational reality is advanced in order to justify a traditional *prescription*. Thus, those who insist that our schools are run by a cabal of constructivists who have turned them into hotbeds of Deweyan progressivism are usually attempting to rationalize the use of even more direct instruction of isolated skills, even less opportunity for students to play an active role in their own learning.

"Back to basics"? When did we ever leave?

I'm not accusing anyone of harboring a sinister desire to make children miserable. I am saying that some people tend to worry an awful lot about the prospect of excessive enjoyment. I suspect that those who dedicate themselves to the task of arresting any real or imagined outbreak of feel-good teaching often believe that if children seem to be happy in school, then not much of value could be going on there.

I call it the Listerine theory of education, based on a famous ad campaign that sought to sell this particular brand of mouthwash on the theory that if it tasted vile, it obviously had to work well. The converse proposition, that anything appealing is likely to be ineffective, is not limited to the realm of schooling. Just as efforts to undermine public education (masquerading as a solemn commitment to leave no child behind) are part of a larger campaign to privatize democratic public institutions, so does an attack on suspiciously enjoyable classroom practices reflect a deeper and wider sensibility. "Feel-good" is an all-purpose epithet, standing ready to disparage almost anything that is too pleasurable.

There's work to be done! Life (or learning, or whatever) isn't supposed to be fun and games! Self-denial—whose adherents generally presume to deny others as well—is closely connected to fear of pleasure and redemption through suffering, and the whole package has a pedigree that is not only philosophical but theological. Who says religion has been banished from the public schools?

There's a clear line of sight to this dogma from a sterile classroom whose children are sweating over worksheets. You can also see it pretty clearly from the administrative offices where people in suits decree the elimination of recess or even build elementary schools without playgrounds.

The irony is, appropriately enough, painful: Academic excellence, the usual rationale for such decisions, is actually far more likely to flourish when students enjoy what they're doing. "Children (and adults, too) learn best when they are happy," as Nel Noddings observes in her book *Happiness and Education*. How they feel—about themselves, about their teachers, about the curriculum and the whole experience of school—is crucially related to the quality of their learning. Richer thinking is more likely to occur in an atmosphere of exuberant discovery, in the kind of place where kids plunge into their projects and can't wait to pick up where they left off yesterday.

Numerous studies have demonstrated how interest drives achievement—ongoing interest in a general topic more than transient interest in a specific activity, and excited interest more than the casual, mild kind. Regardless of age, race, or aptitude, students are more likely to remember and really understand what they've read if they find it intriguing. The interest level of the text, in fact, is a much better predictor of what students will get out of it than its difficulty level. (Incidentally, the same general connection between affect and achievement shows up with adults, too. After all, how do we expect to attract and retain good teachers when neither they nor those whom they teach have much occasion to smile?)

But in pointing this out, I fear that I'm appearing to accept an odious premise—namely, that joy must be justified as a means to the end of better academic performance. Not so: It's an end in itself. Not the only end, perhaps, but a damned important one. Thus, anyone who has spent time in classrooms that vibrate with enthusiasm needs to keep such memories alive in all their specificity to serve as so many yardsticks against which to measure what we've lost: six-year-olds listening to a story, rapt and breathless; teenagers so immersed in an activity that they forget to worry about appearing cool; those little explosions of delight attendant on figuring something out.

I am convinced that historians will look back at our era of ever-higher standards and increasingly standardized instruction as a dark period in American education. What were we thinking, they will ask, shaking their heads, when we begrudged children the right to spend their days in a place that provides deep satisfactions and occasional giggles? How did we allow this to happen?

In a news report about what has been stripped away from children's education in order that they can spend more time on test preparation, a spokesman for a large school district defended such policies on the grounds that they were handed down from above. "We haven't had recess in years," he acknowledged. "They say this is the way it's going to be, and we say, 'Fine.'"

Why are our schools not places of joy? Because too many of us respond to outrageous edicts by saying, "Fine."

13.   Against "Competitiveness"

Here are some phrases that might reassure us if they were used to defend a particular education policy: "excitement about learning" . . . "deeper thinking about questions that matter" . . . "promoting social and moral development" . . . "democratic society."

And here's a phrase that ought to make us wince and back away slowly: "competitiveness in a twenty-first-century global economy."

For years, champions of high-stakes testing and mandatory curriculum standards have invoked a need to ratchet up the skills of future employees and, by extension, the revenues of U.S. corporations. Now, though, *opponents* of such policies are using the identical argument. In recent months, two prominent critics of No Child Left Behind have argued in separate articles that the law's effect on instruction isn't consistent with what's needed to produce successful workers.

I'm sure they're right. But just as we shouldn't justify a wonderful curriculum by claiming it will raise standardized test scores—first, because such tests measure what matters least, and second, because claims of this sort serve to legitimate these tests—so we should hesitate to defend or criticize educational practices on economic grounds.

Various strands of evidence have converged to challenge the claim that the state of our economy is a function of how good our schools are at preparing tomorrow's workers. For individual students, school achievement is only weakly related to subsequent workplace performance. And for nations, there's little correlation between average test scores and economic vigor.

Schools make a tempting scapegoat when a company's financial results are disappointing or when the economy as a whole falters. But an employee's educational background is only one of many factors that determine his or her productivity. Worker productivity, in turn, is only one of many factors that determine corporate profitability. And corporate profitability is only one of many factors that determine the state of the economy—particularly the employment picture. Does anyone seriously believe, for example, that the main reason U.S. companies are shipping jobs by the millions to Mexico and Asia is because they believe those countries' schools are better?

But let's talk about values, not just facts. Is the main mission of schools really to prepare children to be productive workers who will do their part to increase the profitability of their future employers? Every time education is described as an "investment," or schools are discussed in the context of the "global economy," a loud alarm ought to go off, reminding us of the moral and practical implications of giving an answer in dollars to a question about schools. As Jonathan Kozol recently reminded us, good teachers "refuse to see their pupils as . . . pint-sized deficits or assets for America's economy into whom they are expected to pump 'added value.'"

Lending an even more noxious twist to the habit of seeing education in purely economic terms is the use of the word "competitiveness," which implies that our goals should be framed in terms of beating others rather than doing well. When the topic is globalization, it's commonly assumed that competition is unavoidable: For one enterprise (or country) to succeed, another must fail. But even if this were true—and economists Paul Krugman and the late David Gordon have separately argued it probably isn't—why in the world would we accept the same zero-sum mentality with respect to learning?

Consider the sport of ranking the United States against other nations on standardized tests. Once we've debunked the myth that test scores predict economic success, why would we worry about our country's standing as measured by those scores? To say that our students are first, or tenth, on a list provides no useful information about how much they know or how good our schools are. If all the countries did reasonably well in absolute terms, there would be no shame in (and, perhaps, no statistical significance to) being at the bottom. If all the countries did poorly, there would be no glory in being at the top. Exclamatory headlines about how "our" schools are doing compared to "theirs" suggest that we're less concerned with the quality of education than with whether we can chant, "We're Number One!"

An essay published [in *Education Week*] in 2006 reported that U.S. students are doing better in mathematics than earlier generations did. Was the author moved by this fact to express delight, or at least relief? On the contrary, he pronounced the current state of affairs "disturbing" because children in other countries are also doing well—and that, by definition, is considered bad news.

Likewise, the *New York Times* warned in the late 1990s that "American high school graduation rates, for generations the highest in the world, have slipped below those of most industrialized countries." Actually, on most measures, the United States is doing better than ever in terms of the proportion of our adults who finish school. But again we were invited to fret because progress had been made by other countries, too, meaning we were no longer king of the mountain.

What if we just ignored the status of students in other countries? That wouldn't be especially neighborly, but at least we wouldn't be viewing the gains of children in other lands as a troubling development. Better yet, rather than defending whatever policies will ostensibly help our graduates to "compete," we could make decisions on the basis of what will help them *collaborate* effectively. Educators, too, might think in terms of working with—and learning from—their counterparts in other countries.

Even beyond the moral justification for transcending reflexive rivalry, Janet Swenson at Michigan State University points out that "we'll all benefit from the best education we can provide to every child on the face of this planet. Do you care if it's a child in Africa who finds a cure for cancer rather than a child in your country?" she asks.

It took me awhile to realize that at the core of the current "tougher standards" movement is a worldview characterized by artificial scarcity—along with the assumption that schooling is ultimately about economic outcomes. A more reasonable and humane perspective is always hard to come by when we're told that we're in a race. The prospects for critical thought are particularly bleak if the race never ends.

Sadder still, the same competitive mindset shows up as district is pitted against district, school against school, student against student. Several years ago, one superintendent in the Northeast vowed that his city's test scores would "never be last again" in his state. Like so many others, he was confusing higher scores with better learning. But this appalling statement also implied that his students didn't have to improve; so long as kids in another community fared even more poorly, he would be satisfied. Such a position is not only intellectually indefensible (because of its focus on *relative* performance) but morally bankrupt (because of its indifference to the welfare of children in other places).

Almost any policy, it seems, no matter how harmful, can be rationalized in the name of "competitiveness" by politicians and corporate executives, or by journalists whose imaginations are flatter than the world about which they write. But educators ought to aim higher. Our loyalty, after all, is not to corporations but to children. Our chief concern—our "bottom line," if you must—is not victory for some, but learning for all.

14. When Twenty-First-Century Schooling Just Isn't Good Enough: A Modest Proposal

Many school administrators, and even more people who aren't educators but are kind enough to offer their advice about how our field can be improved, have emphasized the need for "twenty-first-century schools" that teach "twenty-first-century skills." But is this really enough, particularly now that our adversaries (in other words, people who live in other countries) may be thinking along the same lines? Unfortunately, no. Beginning immediately, therefore, we must begin to implement *twenty-second*-century education.

What does that phrase mean? How can we possibly know what skills will be needed so far in the future? Such challenges from skeptics—the same kind of people who ask annoying questions about other cutting-edge ideas, including "brain-based education"—are to be expected. But if we're confident enough to describe what education should be like throughout the twenty-first century—that is, what will be needed over the next ninety years or so—it's not much of a stretch to reach a few decades beyond that.

Essentially, we can take whatever objectives or teaching strategies we happen to favor and, merely by attaching a label that designates a future time period, endow them (and ourselves) with an aura of novelty and significance. Better yet, we instantly define our critics as impediments to progress. If this trick works for the adjective "twenty-first-century," imagine the payoff from ratcheting it up by a hundred years.

To describe schooling as twenty-second-century, however, does suggest a somewhat specific agenda. First, it signifies an emphasis on competitiveness. Even those who talk about twenty-first-century schools invariably follow that phrase with a reference to "the need to compete in a global economy." The goal isn't excellence, in other words; it's victory. Education is first and foremost about being first

 Originally published in *District Administration*, February 2009

and foremost. Therefore, we might as well trump the twenty-first-century folks by peering even further into the future.

You may have noticed the connection between this conception of education and the practice of continually ranking students on the basis of their scores on standardized tests. This is a promising start, but it doesn't go nearly far enough. Twenty-*second*-century schooling means that just about everything should be evaluated in terms of who's beating whom. Thus, newspapers might feature headlines like: "U.S. Schools Now in 4th Place in Number of Hall Monitors" or "Gates Funds $50-Billion Effort to Manufacture World-Class Cafeteria Trays." Whatever the criterion, our challenge is to make sure that people who don't live in the United States will always be inferior to us.

This need to be number one also explains why we can no longer settle for teaching the "whole child." The trouble is that if you have a whole of something, you have only one of it. From now on, therefore, you can expect to see conferences devoted to educating a "child-and-a-half" (CAAH). Nothing less will do in a twenty-second-century global—or possibly interplanetary—economy. To cite the title of a forthcoming best-seller that educators will be reading in place of dusty tomes about pedagogy, *The Solar System Is Flat*.

In addition to competitiveness, those who specify an entire century to frame their objectives tend not to be distracted by all the fretting about what's good for children. Instead, they ask, "What do our *corporations* need?" and work backwards from there. We must never forget the primary reason that children attend school—namely, to be trained in the skills that will maximize the profits earned by their future employers. Indeed, we have already made great strides in shifting the conversation about education to what will prove useful in workplaces rather than wasting time discussing what might support "democracy" (an eighteenth-century notion, isn't it?) or what might promote self development as an intrinsic good (a concept that goes back thousands of years and is therefore antiquated by definition).

How can we redouble our commitment to business-oriented

schooling? If necessary, we can outsource some of the learning to students in Asia, who will memorize more facts for lower grades. And we can complete the process, already begun in spirit, of making universities' education departments subsidiaries of their business schools. More generally, we must put an end to pointless talk about students' "interest" in learning and instead focus on skills that will contribute to the bottom line. Again, we're delighted to report that this shift is already underway, thanks to those who keep reminding us about the importance of twenty-first-century schooling.

This is no time for complacency, though. Not everyone is on board yet, and that means we'll have to weed out teachers whose stubborn attachment to less efficient educational strategies threatens to slow down the engine of our future economy. How can we rid our schools of those who refuse to be team players? Well, we can insist that all classroom instruction be rigorously aligned to state standards—a very effective technique since most of those standards documents were drafted by people steeped in the models, methods, and metaphors of corporations. We can also use merit pay to enforce compliance by stigmatizing anyone who doesn't play by the new rules. (Come to think of it, here, too, we're already well on our way to creating twenty-second-century classrooms.)

The final distinguishing feature of education that's geared to the next century is its worshipful attitude toward mathematics and technology. "If you can't quantify it or plug it in, who needs it?" Of course, the reason we will continue to redirect resources toward math and science (and away from literature and the arts) isn't because the former are inherently more important but simply because they're more useful from an economic standpoint. And that standpoint is the only one that matters for schools with a proper twenty-second-century mindset.

One last point. We will of course continue to talk earnestly about the need for a curriculum that features "critical thinking" skills—by which we mean the specific proficiencies acceptable to CEOs. But you will appreciate the need to delicately discourage *real* critical thinking on the part of students, since this might lead them to pose inconvenient questions about the entire enterprise and the ideology on which it's based. There's certainly no room for *that* in the global competitive economy of the future. Or the present.

Alfie Kohn has recently completed a book called Crime and Punishment. *He expects to begin reading another one shortly.*

15. Debunking the Case for National Standards

I keep thinking it can't get much worse, and then it does. Throughout the 1990s, one state after another adopted prescriptive education standards enforced by frequent standardized testing, often of the high-stakes variety. A top-down, get-tough movement to impose "accountability"—driven more by political than educational considerations—began to squeeze the life out of classrooms, doing the most damage in the poorest areas.

By the time the century ended, many of us thought we had hit bottom—until the floor gave way and we found ourselves in a basement we didn't know existed. I'm referring, of course, to what should have been called the Many Children Left Behind Act, which requires every state to test every student every year, judging students and schools almost exclusively by their scores on those tests, and hurting the schools that need the most help. Ludicrously unrealistic proficiency targets suggest that the law was actually intended to sabotage rather than improve public education.

Today we survey the wreckage. Talented teachers have abandoned the profession after having been turned into glorified test-prep technicians. Low-income teenagers have been forced out of school by do-or-die graduation exams. Countless inventive learning activities have been eliminated in favor of prefabricated lessons pegged to numbingly specific state standards.

And now we're informed that what we really need . . . is to standardize this whole operation from coast to coast.

Have we lost our minds? Because we're certainly in the process of losing our children's minds.

To politicians, corporate CEOs, or companies that produce standardized tests, this prescription may seem to make sense. (Notice that this is exactly the cast of characters leading the initiative for national standards.) But if you spend your days with real kids in real

 Originally published in *Education Week*, January 14, 2010

classrooms, you're more likely to find yourself wondering how much longer those kids—and the institution of public education—can survive this accountability fad.

Let's be clear about the latest development. First, what they're trying to sell us are national standards. It may be politically expedient to insist that the effort isn't driven by the federal government, but if all, or nearly all, states end up adopting the same mandates, that distinction doesn't amount to much.

Second, these core standards will inevitably be accompanied by a national standardized test. When asked during an online chat whether that was true, Dane Linn of the National Governors Association (a key player in this initiative) didn't deny it. "Standards alone," he replied, "will not drive teaching and learning"—meaning, of course, the specific type of teaching and learning that the authorities require. Even if we took the advice of the late Harold Howe II, former U.S. Commissioner of Education, and made the standards "as vague as possible," a national test creates a de facto national curriculum, particularly if high stakes are attached.

Third, a relatively small group of experts will be designing standards, test questions, and curricula for the rest of us based on their personal assumptions about what it means to be well educated. The official Core Standards Web site tries to deny this, insisting that the items all teachers are going to have to teach will be "based on evidence" rather than reflecting "individual beliefs about what is important." It would be charitable to describe this claim as disingenuous. Evidence can tell us whether a certain method is effective for reaching a certain objective—for example, how instruction aligned to this standard will affect a score on that test. But the selection of the goal itself—what our children will be taught and tested on—unavoidably reflects values and beliefs. Should those of a single group of individuals determine what happens in every public school in the country?

Advocates of national standards tell us they want all students (by which they mean only American students) to attain excellence, no matter where (in our country) they happen to live. The problem is that excellence is being confused with entirely different attributes, such as uniformity, rigor, specificity, and victory. Let's consider each in turn.

Are all kids entitled to a great education? Of course. But that doesn't mean all kids should get the *same* education. High standards don't require common standards. Uniformity is not the same thing as excellence—or equity. (In fact, one-size-fits-all demands may offer the illusion of fairness, setting back the cause of genuine equity.) To acknowledge these simple truths is to watch the rationale for national standards—or uniform state standards—collapse into a heap of intellectual rubble.

To be sure, excellence and uniformity might turn out to be empirically correlated even if they're theoretically distinct. But I know of no evidence that students in countries as diverse as ours with national standards or curricula engage in unusually deep thinking or are particularly excited about learning. Even standardized test results, such as the Trends in International Mathematics and Science Study (TIMSS), provide no support for the nationalizers. On eighth-grade math and science tests, eight of the ten top-scoring countries had centralized education systems, but so did nine of the ten lowest-scoring countries in math and eight of the ten lowest-scoring countries in science.

So if students don't benefit from uniformity, who does? Presumably corporations that sell curriculum materials and tests can reduce their costs if one text fits all. And then there are the policy makers who confuse doing well with beating others. If you're determined to evaluate students or schools in *relative* terms, it helps if they're all doing the same thing. But why would we want to turn learning into a competitive sport?

Apart from the fact that they're unnecessary, a key premise of national standards, as the University of Chicago's Zalman Usiskin observed, is that "our teachers cannot be trusted to make decisions about which curriculum is best for their schools." Moreover, uniformity doesn't just happen—and continue—on its own. To get everyone to apply the same standards, you need top-down control. What happens, then, to educators who disagree with some of the mandates, or with the premise that teaching should be broken into separate disciplines, or with the whole idea of national standards? What are the implications of accepting a system characterized by what Deborah Meier called "centralized power over ideas"?

I've written elsewhere about another error: equating harder with better and making a fetish of "rigorous" demands or tests whose primary virtue (if it's a virtue at all) is that they're really difficult. Read just about any brief for national standards and you'll witness this confusion in full bloom. A key selling point is that we're "raising the bar"—even though, as Voltaire reminded us, "That which is merely difficult gives no pleasure in the end." Nor does it enhance learning.

Then, too, there is a conflation of quality with specificity. If children—and communities—are different from one another, the only safe way to apply an identical standard to all of them is to operate at a high level of abstraction: "We will help all students to communicate effectively," for example. (Hence Howe's enduring wisdom about the need to keep things vague.) The more specific the standard, the more problematic it becomes to impose it on everyone. Pretty soon you're gratuitously defining some kids as failures, particularly if the new standards are broken down by grade level.

The reasonable-sounding adjectives used to defend an agenda of specificity—"focused," "coherent," "precise," "clear"—ought to make us nervous. If standards comprise narrowly defined facts and skills, then we have accepted a controversial model of education, one that consists of transmitting vast quantities of material to students, material that even the most successful may not remember, care about, or be able to use.

This is exactly what most state standards have already become and it's where national standards are heading (even if, in theory, they could be otherwise). Specificity is what business groups and newspaper editorialists want and it's what very vocal defenders of "core

knowledge" equate with good teaching. Specificity is a major criterion by which *Education Week* and conservative think tanks like the
Thomas B. Fordham Institute evaluate standards documents. In any
case, Achieve, Inc. and the National Governors Association probably
won't need much convincing; they'll give us specific in spades.

Finally, what's the *purpose* of demanding that every kid in every
school in every state must be able to do the same thing in the same
year, with teachers pressured to "align" their instruction to a master
curriculum and a standardized test?

I once imagined a drinking game in which a few of those education reform papers from corporate groups and politicians were read
aloud: You take a shot every time you hear "rigorous," "measurable,"
"accountable," "competitive," "world-class," "high(er) expectations,"
or "raising the bar." Within a few minutes, everyone would be so
inebriated that they'd no longer be able to recall a time when discussions about schooling weren't studded with these macho managerial
buzzwords.

But not all jargon is meaningless. Those words actually have very
real implications for what classrooms should look like and what education is (and isn't) all about. The goal clearly isn't to nourish children's curiosity, to help them fall in love with reading and thinking,
to promote both the ability and the disposition to think critically,
or to support a democratic society. Rather, a prescription for uniform, specific, rigorous standards is made to order for those whose
chief concern is to pump up the American economy and make sure
that we triumph over people who live in other countries.

If you read the FAQ page on the common core standards Web
site, don't bother looking for words like "exploration," "intrinsic motivation," "developmentally appropriate," or "democracy."
Instead, the very first sentence contains the phrase "success in the
global economy," followed immediately by "America's competitive
edge."

If these bright new digitally enhanced national standards are more economic than educational in their inspiration, more about winning than learning, devoted more to serving the interests of business than to meeting the needs of kids, then we've merely painted a twenty-first-century façade on a hoary, dreary model of school as employee training. Anyone who recoils from that vision should be doing everything possible to resist a proposal for national standards that embodies it.

Yes, we want excellent teaching and learning for all—although our emphasis should be less on *student achievement* (read: test scores) than on *students' achievements*. Offered a list of standards, we should scrutinize each one but also ask who came up with them and for what purpose. Is there room for discussion and disagreement—and not just by experts—regarding what, and how, we're teaching and how authentic our criteria are for judging success? Or is this a matter of "obey or else," with tests to enforce compliance?

The standards movement, sad to say, morphed long ago into a push for standardization. The last thing we need is more of the same.

Five: Beyond the Schools

Psychological Issues & Parenting

16. Atrocious Advice from Supernanny

A despot welcomes a riot. Disorder provides an excuse to rescind liberties in order to restore calm. There are only two choices, after all: chaos and control. Even the creators of *Get Smart* understood that.

And so, too, do the creators of *Supernanny* and *Nanny 911*. Each week they poke their cameras into a dysfunctional suburban home where the children are bouncing off the walls and the parents are ready to climb them. There's whining, there's yelling, there's hitting . . . and the kids are just as bad. But wait. Look up there: It's a bird. It's a plain-dressed, no-nonsense British nanny, poised to swoop in with a prescription for old-fashioned control. Soon the clueless American parents will be comfortably back in charge, the children will be calm and compliant, and everyone will be sodden with gratitude. Cue the syrupy music, the slo-mo hugs, the peek at next week's even more hopeless family.

These programs elevate viewer manipulation to an art form. For starters, the selection of unusually obnoxious children invites us to enjoy a shiver of self-congratulation: At least my kids—and my parenting skills—aren't that bad! More to the point, these anarchic families set us up to root for totalitarian solutions. Anything to stop the rioting.

We're encouraged to pretend that living with a camera crew doesn't influence how parents and children interact, and to disregard what it says about these people that they allowed their humiliation to be televised. We're asked to believe that families can be utterly transformed in a few days and to assume that the final redemptive images reveal the exceptional skills of the nanny—rather than of the program's editing staff. By now, a fair number of TV dramas, and even some sitcoms, refrain from serving up contrived happy endings. Sometimes the patient dies, the perp outwits the prosecutor, the jerk is unreformed. Yet here, in the realm of nonfiction programming, a tidy solution must be found before signoff. Perhaps it's reality television that's most divorced from reality.

We might just laugh off the implausibility of these programs except that they're teaching millions of real parents how to raise their real kids. To that extent, it matters that they're selling snake oil.

Consider ABC's *Supernanny*. (Fox's copycat *Nanny 911* differs mostly in that a rotating cast of nannies shares top billing.) The show is rigidly formulaic: Jo Frost, the titular nanny and now bestselling author, arrives, observes, grimaces, states the obvious, imposes a schedule along with a set of rules and punishments. The parents stumble but then get the hang of her system. Contentment ensues.

The limits of the show, however, are less consequential than the limits of its star. Ms. Frost's approach to family crises is stunningly simple-minded; it's the narrowness of her repertoire, not merely the constraints of the medium, that leads her to ignore the important questions. She never stops to ask whether the demands of work and kids could be more gracefully reconciled if high-quality, low-cost daycare was available. She doesn't even inquire into psychological issues. Are the parents' expectations appropriate for the age of the child? Might something deeper than a lack of skills explain why they respond, or fail to respond, to their children as they do? How were *they* raised?

The nanny never peers below the surface, and her analysis of every family is identical. The problem is always that the parents aren't sufficiently vigorous in controlling their children. She has no reservations about power so long as only the big people have it. Kids are the enemy to be conquered. (At the beginning of *Nanny 911*, the stentorian narrator warns of tots "taking over the household"; the children in one episode are described as "little monsters.") Parents learn how to get them to take their naps *now*. Whether the kids are tired is irrelevant.

Supernanny's favorite words are "technique" and "consistency." First, a schedule is posted—they will all eat at six o'clock because she says so—and the children are given a list of generic rules. The point is enforcement and order, not teaching and reflection. Thus, rather than helping a child to think about the effects of his aggression on others, he is simply informed that hitting is "unacceptable"; reasons and morality don't enter into it. Then he is forced to "stand in the naughty corner." Later, the nanny instructs Dad to command the child to apologize. The desired words are muttered under duress. The adults seem pleased.

For balance, kids are controlled with rewards as well as with punishments. Those who haven't been eating what (or when, or as much as) the parent wishes are slathered with praise as soon as they do so—a "Good boy!" for every mouthful. Sure enough, they fork in some more food. These children may be so desperate for acceptance that they settle for contingent reinforcement in place of the unconditional love they really need.

The little girl in one family is accustomed to having Mom lie down next to her at bedtime. Forget it, says Supernanny, and the tradition is ended without warning or explanation. When the girl screams, that only proves how manipulative she is. Later, Mom confesses, "I felt like I was almost mistreating her." "Do not give in," urges the nanny, and misgivings soon yield to "It's working; it's getting quieter"—meaning that her daughter has abandoned hope that Mom will snuggle with her.

On another episode, a boy is playing with a hose in the backyard when his mother suddenly announces, "You're done." The boy protests ("I'm cleaning!"), so she turns off the water. He becomes angry and kicks over a wagon. Supernanny is incredulous: "Just because she turned the water off!" There is no comment about the autocratic, disrespectful parenting that precipitated his outburst. But then, autocratic, disrespectful parenting is her stock in trade.

Supernanny's superficiality isn't accidental; it's ideological. What these shows are peddling is behaviorism. The point isn't to raise a child; it's to reinforce or extinguish discrete behaviors—which is sufficient if you believe, along with the late B. F. Skinner and his surviving minions, that there's nothing to us other than those behaviors.

Behaviorism is as American as rewarding children with apple pie.

We're a busy people, with fortunes to make and lands to conquer. We don't have time for theories or complications: Just give us techniques that work. If firing thousands of employees succeeds in boosting the company's stock price; if imposing a scripted, mind-numbing curriculum succeeds in raising students' test scores; if relying on bribes and threats succeeds in making children obey, then there's no need to ask, "But for how long does it work? And at what cost?"

In the course of researching a book called *Unconditional Parenting*, I discovered some disconcerting research on the damaging effects of techniques like the "naughty corner" (better known as time out), which are basically forms of love withdrawal. I also found quite a bit of evidence that parents who refrain from excessive control and rely instead on warmth and reason are more likely to have children who do what they're asked—and who grow into responsible, compassionate, healthy people.

If you can bear to sit through them, the nanny programs provide a fairly reliable guide for how *not* to raise children. They also offer an invitation to think about the pervasiveness of pop-behaviorism and our hunger for the quick fix. "I guarantee you," Supernanny earnestly, if tautologically, exhorts one pair of parents, "every time you're consistent, [your child] gets the same message."

Granted, but what message?

17.   Parental Love with Strings Attached

More than fifty years ago, Carl Rogers suggested that successful psychotherapy relies on three key ingredients. Therapists must be genuine rather than hiding behind a mask of professionalism. They must understand their clients' feelings accurately. And they must put aside judgment in order to express "unconditional positive regard" for those they seek to help.

That last one is a doozy—not only because it's so difficult but because of what the need for it says about how we were raised. Rogers believed that therapists need to accept their clients without any strings attached so that the clients can begin to accept themselves. And the reason so many have disowned or repressed parts of who they are is because their parents put "conditions of worth" on their care: I love you, but only when you're well behaved (or successful in school, or impressive to other adults, or quiet, or thin, or deferential, or cute . . .).

The implication is that loving our children isn't enough. We have to love them unconditionally—for who they are, not for what they do.

As a father, I know this is a tall order, but it becomes even more challenging now that so much of the advice we are given amounts to exactly the opposite. In effect, we're given tips in *conditional* parenting, which comes in two flavors: turn up the affection when they're good, withhold affection when they're not.

Thus, TV's "Dr. Phil" McGraw tells us in his book *Family First* that what children need or enjoy should be offered contingently, turned into rewards to be doled out or withheld so they "behave according to your wishes." And "one of the most powerful currencies for a child," he adds, "is the parents' acceptance and approval."

Likewise, Jo Frost of the TV show *Supernanny,* in her book of the same name, says, "The best rewards are attention, praise, and love," and these should be held back "when the child behaves badly . . . until she says she is sorry," at which point the love is turned back on.

Note that conditional parenting isn't limited to old-school authoritarians. Some people who wouldn't dream of spanking choose instead to discipline their young children by forcibly isolating them, a tactic we prefer to call "time out." Conversely, "positive reinforcement" teaches children that they're loved—and lovable—only when they do whatever we decide is a "good job."

This raises the intriguing possibility that the problem with praise isn't that it is done the wrong way—or handed out too easily, as social conservatives insist. Rather, it might be just another method of control, analogous to punishment. The primary message of all types of conditional parenting is that children must *earn* a parent's love. A steady diet of that, Rogers warned, and children might eventually need a therapist to provide the unconditional acceptance they didn't get when it counted.

But was Rogers right? Before we toss out mainstream discipline, it would be nice to have some evidence. And now we do.

In 2004, two Israeli researchers, Avi Assor and Guy Roth, joined Edward Deci, a leading American expert on the psychology of motivation, in asking more than one hundred college students whether the love they had received from their parents had seemed to depend on whether they had succeeded in school, practiced hard for sports, been considerate toward others, or suppressed emotions like anger and fear.

It turned out that children who received conditional approval were indeed somewhat more likely to act as the parent wanted. But compliance came at a steep price. First, these children tended to resent and dislike their parents. Second, they were apt to say that the way they acted was often due more to a "strong internal pressure" than to "a real sense of choice." Moreover, their happiness after succeeding at something was usually short-lived, and they often felt guilty or ashamed.

In a companion study, Assor and his colleagues interviewed a group of mothers of grown children. With this generation, too, conditional parenting proved damaging. Those mothers who, as children, sensed that they were loved only when they lived up to their parents' expectations now felt less worthy as adults. Yet despite the negative effects, these mothers were more likely to use conditional affection with their own children.

In 2009, the same researchers, now joined by two of Deci's colleagues at the University of Rochester, published two replications and extensions of the 2004 study. This time their subjects were ninth graders, and this time giving more attention and affection when children did what parents wanted was carefully distinguished from giving less when they did not.

The studies found that both positive and negative conditional parenting were harmful, but in slightly different ways. The positive kind sometimes succeeded in getting children to work harder on academic tasks, but at the cost of unhealthy feelings of "internal compulsion." Negative conditional parenting, meanwhile, didn't even work in the short run; it just increased the teenagers' negative feelings about their parents.

What these—and other—studies tell us, if we're able to hear the news, is that praising children for doing something right isn't a meaningful alternative to pulling back or punishing when they do something wrong. Both are examples of conditional parenting, and both are counterproductive.

The child psychologist Bruno Bettelheim, who readily acknowledged that the version of negative conditional parenting known as time out can cause "deep feelings of anxiety," nevertheless endorsed it for that very reason. "When our words are not enough," he said, "the threat of the withdrawal of our love and affection is the only sound method to impress on him that he had better conform to our request."

But the data suggest that love withdrawal isn't particularly effective at getting compliance, much less at promoting moral development. Even if we did succeed in making children obey us, though—say, by using positive reinforcement—is obedience worth the possible long-term psychological harm? Should parental love be used as a tool for controlling children?

Deeper issues also underlie a different sort of criticism. Albert Bandura, the father of the branch of psychology known as social learning theory, declared that unconditional love "would make children directionless and quite unlovable"—an assertion entirely unsupported by empirical studies. The idea that children accepted for who they are would lack direction or appeal is most informative for what it tells us about the dark view of human nature held by those who issue such warnings.

In practice, according to an impressive collection of data by Deci and others, unconditional acceptance by parents as well as teachers should be accompanied by "autonomy support": explaining reasons for requests, maximizing opportunities for the child to participate in making decisions, being encouraging without manipulating, and actively imagining how things look from the child's point of view.

The last of these features is important with respect to unconditional parenting itself. Most of us would protest that of course we love our children without any strings attached. But what counts is how things look from the perspective of the children—whether they feel just as loved when they mess up or fall short.

Carl Rogers didn't say so, but I'll bet he would have been glad to see less demand for skillful therapists if that meant more people were growing into adulthood having already felt unconditionally accepted.

18. Why Self-Discipline Is Overrated: The (Troubling) Theory and Practice of Control from Within

If there is one character trait whose benefits are endorsed by traditional and progressive educators alike, it may well be self-discipline. Just about everyone wants students to override their unconstructive impulses, resist temptation, and do what needs to be done. True, this disposition is commended to us with particular fervor by the sort of folks who sneer at any mention of self-esteem and deplore what they insist are today's lax standards. But even people who don't describe themselves as conservative agree that imposing discipline on children (either to improve their behavior or so they'll apply themselves to their studies) isn't nearly as desirable as having children discipline themselves. It's appealing to teachers—indeed, to anyone in a position of relative power—if the people over whom they have authority will do what they're supposed to do on their own. The only question is how best to accomplish this.

Self-discipline might be defined as marshalling one's willpower to accomplish things that are generally regarded as desirable, and *self-control* as using that same sort of willpower to prevent oneself from doing what is seen to be *un*desirable or to delay gratification. In practice, these often function as two aspects of the same machinery of self-regulation, so I'll use the two terms more or less interchangeably. Do a search for them in indexes of published books, scholarly articles, or Internet sites, and you'll quickly discover how rare it is to find a discouraging word, or even a penetrating question, about their value.

While I readily admit that it's good to be able to persevere at worthwhile tasks—and that some students seem to lack this capacity—I want to suggest that the concept is actually problematic in three fundamental ways. To inquire into what underlies the idea of self-discipline is to uncover serious misconceptions about motivation and personality, controversial assumptions about human nature, and disturbing implications regarding how things are arranged in a classroom or a society. Let's call these challenges *psychological, philosophical,* and *political,* respectively. All of them apply to self-discipline in general, but they're particularly relevant to what happens in our schools.

I. PSYCHOLOGICAL ISSUES: Critical Distinctions

If our main goal for students is just to get them to complete whatever tasks, and obey whatever rules, they're given, then self-discipline is undeniably a useful trait. But if we're interested in the whole child—if, for example, we'd like our students to be psychologically healthy—then it's not at all clear that self-discipline should enjoy a privileged status compared to other attributes. In some contexts, it may not be desirable at all.

Several decades ago, the eminent research psychologist Jack Block described people in terms of their level of "ego control"—that is, the extent to which impulses and feelings are expressed or suppressed. Those who are undercontrolled are impulsive and distractible; those who are overcontrolled are compulsive and joyless. The fact that educators are more irritated by the former, and thus more likely to define it as a problem, doesn't mean the latter is any less troubling. Nor should we favor "the replacement of unbridled impulsivity with categorical, pervasive, rigid impulse control," Block warned. It's not just that self-control isn't always good; it's that a *lack* of self-control isn't always bad because it may "provide the basis for spontaneity, flexibility, expressions of interpersonal warmth, openness to experience, and creative recognitions." So what does it say about our society that "the idea of self-control is generally praised" even though it may sometimes be "maladaptive and spoil the experience and savorings of life"?[1]

The idea that either extreme can be unwise shouldn't be particularly controversial, yet the possibility of unhealthy overcontrol is explicitly rejected by some researchers who double as cheerleaders for self-discipline.[2] Moreover, a reluctance to acknowledge this important caution is apparent in the array of published materials on the subject. Such discussions typically contain unqualified assertions such as "The promotion of self-discipline is an important goal for all schools" or "Teaching self discipline to students should be something all teachers strive for."[3]

It's hard to square those statements with research that finds "disciplined and directed behavior, which can be advantageous in some situations. . . . is likely to be detrimental" in others.[4] Not only has it been shown that "the consequences of impulsivity are not always negative,"[5] but a high degree of self-control tends to go hand-in-hand with less spontaneity and a blander emotional life[6]—and, in some cases, with more serious psychological problems.[7] "Overcontrollers tend to be complete abstainers from drug use, but they are less well adjusted than individuals who have lower ego control and may have experimented briefly with drugs, [while] a tendency toward overcontrol puts young women (but not young men) at risk for the development of depression."[8] A preoccupation with self-control is also a key feature of anorexia.[9]

Consider a student who always starts her homework the moment it's assigned. What might look like an admirable display of self-discipline, given that there are other things she'd rather be doing, may actually be due to an acute discomfort with having anything unfinished. She wants—or, more accurately, *needs*—to get the assignment out of the way in order to stave off anxiety. (The fact that something resembling self-discipline is required to complete a task doesn't bode well for the likelihood of deriving any intellectual benefit from it. Learning, after all, depends not on what students do so much as on how they regard and construe what they do.[10] To assume otherwise is to revert to a crude behaviorism long since repudiated by serious scholars.)

More generally, self-discipline can be less a sign of health than of vulnerability. It may reflect a fear of being overwhelmed by external forces, or by one's own desires, that must be suppressed through continual effort. In effect, such individuals suffer from a fear of being *out* of control. In his classic work *Neurotic Styles,* David Shapiro described how someone might function as "his own overseer, issuing commands, directives, reminders, warnings, and admonitions concerning not only what is to be done and what is not to be done, but also what is to be wanted, felt, and even thought."[11] Secure, healthy people can be playful, flexible, open to new experiences and self-discovery, deriving satisfaction from the process rather than always focused on the product. An extremely self-disciplined student, by contrast, may see reading or problem-solving purely as a means to the end of a good test score or a high grade. In Shapiro's more general formulation, such people "do not feel comfortable with any activity that lacks an aim or a purpose beyond its own pleasure, and usually they do not recognize the possibility of finding life satisfying without a continuous sense of purpose and effort."[12]

A couple of interesting paradoxes follow from this analysis. One is that while self-discipline implies an exercise of the will, and therefore a free choice, many such people are actually not free at all, psychologically speaking. It's not that they've disciplined themselves so much as that they can't allow themselves to be undisciplined. Likewise for the deferral of gratification, as one researcher observed: Those who put off the payoff "were not just 'better' at self-control, but in a sense they seemed to be unable to avoid it."[13]

A second paradox is that impressive self-discipline may contain the seeds of its own undoing: an explosive failure of control, which psychologists call "disinhibition." From one unhealthy extreme (even if it's not always recognized as such), people may suddenly find themselves at the other: The compliant student abruptly acts out in appalling fashion; the pious teetotaler goes on a dangerous drinking binge; the determined celibate shifts from absolute abstinence to reckless, unprotected sex.[14] Moreover, making an effort to inhibit potentially undesirable behaviors can have other negative effects. A detailed review of research concerning all sorts of attempts to suppress feelings and behaviors concludes that the results often include "negative affect (discomfort or distress) [and] cognitive disruption (including distractibility and intrusive, obsessive thoughts about the proscribed behavior)."[15]

In short, we shouldn't always be reassured to learn that a student is remarkably self-disciplined, or apt to delay gratification (since delayers "tend to be somewhat overcontrolled and unnecessarily inhibited"[16]), or always inclined to persist at a task even when he or she is unsuccessful. The last of these tendencies, commonly romanticized as tenacity or "grit," may actually reflect a "refusal to disengage" that stems from an unhealthy and often counterproductive need to continue with something even when it clearly doesn't make sense to do so.[17]

Of course, not every child who exhibits self-discipline, or something similar, is doing so in a worrisome way. So what distinguishes the healthy and adaptive kind? Moderation, perhaps, but also flexibility, which Block calls "adaptively responsive variability."[18] What counts is the capacity to choose whether and when to persevere, to control oneself, to follow the rules—rather than the simple tendency to do these things in every situation. This, rather than self-discipline or self-control per se, is what children would benefit from developing. But such a formulation is very different from the uncritical celebration of self-discipline that we find in the field of education and throughout our culture.

It's becoming clearer that what can be problematic about self-discipline isn't just a matter of how much but what kind. One of the most fruitful ways of thinking about this issue emerges from the work of motivational psychologists Edward Deci and Richard Ryan. To begin with, they invite us to reconsider the casual way that we talk about the concept of motivation, as if it were a single thing that one possessed in a certain quantity. We want students to have more, so we try to "motivate" them—perhaps with the strategic use of rewards or punishments.

In fact, though, there are different types of motivation, and the type matters more than the amount. *Intrinsic* motivation consists of wanting to do something for its own sake—to read, for example, just because it's exciting to lose oneself in a story. *Extrinsic* motivation exists when the task isn't really the point; one might read in order to get a prize or someone's approval. Not only are these two kinds of motivation different—they tend to be inversely related. Scores of studies have shown that the more you reward people for doing something, the more they're apt to lose interest in whatever they had to do to get the reward. Researchers keep finding that offering children "positive reinforcement" for being helpful and generous ends up undermining those very qualities, and encouraging students to improve their grades results in their becoming less interested in learning.[19]

Yet children do some things that aren't intrinsically appealing even in the absence of extrinsic inducements. They have, we might say, *internalized* a commitment to doing them. And here we return to the idea of self-discipline (with the emphasis on "self"). Indeed, this is exactly where many educators have placed their bets: We want kids to get busy without an adult's having to stand next to them, carrots and sticks at the ready; we want them to act responsibly even when no one is watching.

But Deci and Ryan are not finished complicating our lives. Having shown that there are different kinds of motivation (which are not equally desirable), they go on to suggest that there are also different kinds of internalization (ditto). This is a possibility that few of us have considered; even an educator who can distinguish intrinsic from extrinsic will insist that children should be helped to internalize good values or behaviors, period. But what exactly is the nature of that internalization? On the one hand, a rule or standard can be swallowed whole, or "introjected," so that it controls children from the inside: "Behaviors are performed because one 'should' do them, or because not doing so might engender anxiety, guilt, or loss of esteem." On the other hand, internalization can take place more authentically, so the behavior is experienced as "volitional or self-determined." It's been fully integrated into one's value structure and feels chosen.

Thus, a student may study either because she knows she's supposed to (and will feel lousy about herself if she doesn't), or because she understands the benefits of doing so and wants to follow through even if it's not always pleasurable.[20] This basic distinction has proved relevant to academics, sports, romantic love, generosity, political involvement, and religion—with research in each case demonstrating that the latter kind of internalization leads to better outcomes than the former. With education in particular, it's possible for teachers to promote the more positive version by minimizing "externally imposed evaluations, goals, rewards, and pressures" as well as proactively supporting students' sense of autonomy."[21]

The moral of this story is that just because motivation is internal doesn't mean it's ideal. If kids feel controlled, even from within, they're likely to be conflicted, unhappy, and perhaps less likely to succeed (at least by meaningful criteria) at whatever they're doing. Dutiful students may be suffering from what the psychoanalyst Karen Horney famously called the "tyranny of the should"—to the point that they no longer know what they really want, or who they really are. So it is for teenagers who have mortgaged their present lives to the future: noses to the grindstone, perseverant to a fault, stressed to the max. High school is just preparation for college, and college consists of collecting credentials for whatever comes next. Nothing has any value, or provides any gratification, in itself. These students may be skilled test-takers and grade grubbers and gratification delayers, but they remind us just how mixed the blessing of self-discipline can be.

II. PHILOSOPHICAL ISSUES: Underlying Beliefs

In light of all these reasons for caution, why do we find ourselves so infatuated with self-discipline and self-control? The answer may involve basic values that pervade our culture. Let's ask a different question: What must be true about children—or people in general—if self-discipline is required to make oneself do valuable things?

Consider this recent reflection by David Brooks, a conservative newspaper columnist:

> In Lincoln's day, to achieve maturity was to succeed in the conquest of the self. Human beings were born with sin, inflected with dark passions and satanic temptations. The

transition to adulthood consisted of achieving mastery over them. You can read commencement addresses from the 19th and early 20th centuries in which the speakers would talk about the beast within and the need for iron character to subdue it. Schoolhouse readers emphasized self-discipline. The whole character-building model was sin-centric.[22]

Brooks has it right, with one important caveat: The emphasis on self-discipline isn't just an historical relic. These days we're spared the florid and exhortatory rhetoric, but a few minutes online reminds us that the concept itself is alive and well in contemporary America—to the tune of 3 million hits on Google. (It's also a key element in the character education movement.[23]) Brooks offers a useful if disconcerting reminder about the sin-centric assumptions on which the gospel of self-discipline (still) rests. It's because our preferences are regarded as unworthy, our desires as shameful, that we must strive to overcome them. Taken to its logical conclusion, human life is a constant struggle to stifle and transcend ourselves. Morality consists of the triumph of mind over body, reason over desire, will over want.[24]

What's interesting about all this is how many secular institutions and liberal individuals, who would strenuously object to the notion that children are self-centered little beasts that need to be tamed, nevertheless embrace a concept that springs from just such a premise. Some even make a point of rejecting old-fashioned coercion and punishment in favor of gentler methods.[25] But if they're nevertheless engaged in ensuring that children internalize our values—in effect, by installing a policeman inside each child—then they ought to admit that this isn't the same thing as helping them to develop their own values, and it's diametrically opposed to the goal of helping them to become independent thinkers. Control from within isn't inherently more humane than control from without, particularly if the psychological effects aren't all that different, as it appears they aren't.

Even beyond the vision of human nature, a commitment to self-discipline may reflect a tacit allegiance to philosophical conservatism with its predictable complaint that our society—or its youth—has forgotten the value of hard work, the importance of duty, the need to accept personal responsibility, and so on. (Never mind that older people have been denouncing youthful slackers and "modern times" for centuries.[26]) And this condemnation is typically accompanied by a prescriptive vision that endorses self-denial and sarcastically dismisses talk about self-exploration or self-esteem.

In his fascinating book *Moral Politics,* the linguist and social critic George Lakoff argued that self-discipline plays a critical role in a conservative worldview.[27] Obedience to authority is what produces self-discipline,[28] and self-discipline, in turn, is required for achievement. Its absence is seen as a sign of self-indulgence and therefore of moral weakness. Thus, any time a child receives something desirable, including our approval, without having *earned* it, any time competition is removed (so that success is possible without having to defeat others), any time he or she receives too much assistance or nurturance, then we are being "permissive," "overindulgent," failing to prepare the child for the Real World. Interestingly, this kind of conservatism isn't limited to talk radio or speeches at the Republican convention. It's threaded through the work of key researchers who not only study self-discipline but vigorously insist on its importance.[29]

Of course, fundamental questions about morality and human nature can't be resolved in an article; it's clear that the point of departure for some of us is radically different than it is for others. But for educators who casually invoke the need to teach children self-discipline, it may make sense to explore the philosophical foundation of that concept and to reconsider it if that foundation gives us pause.

III. POLITICAL ISSUES: Practical Implications

When we want to understand what's going on in a given environment—say, a classroom—it often makes sense to look at its policies, norms, and other structural features. Unfortunately, many of us have a tendency to ignore the way the system works and attribute too much significance to the personalities of the individuals involved— a phenomenon that social psychologists have dubbed the fundamental attribution error.[30] Thus, we assume that self-control is just a feature that a person might possess, even though it's probably more accurate to think of it as "a situational concept, not an individual trait" given that "an individual will display different degrees of self-control in different situations." Exactly the same is true of delaying gratification.[31]

It's not just that attending to individuals rather than environments hampers our ability to understand. Doing so also has practical significance. Specifically, the more we fault people for lacking self-discipline and spend our efforts helping them to develop the ability to control their impulses, the less likely we are to question the structures (political, economic, or educational) that shape their actions. There is no reason to work for social change if we assume that people just need to buckle down and try harder. Thus, the attention paid to self-discipline is not only philosophically conservative in its premises, but also politically conservative in its consequences.

Our society is teeming with examples. If consumers are over their heads in debt, the effect of framing the problem as a lack of self-control is to deflect attention from the concerted efforts of the credit industry to get us hooked on borrowing money from the time we're children.[32] Or consider the "Keep America Beautiful" campaign launched in the 1950s that urged us to stop being litterbugs—a campaign financed, it turns out, by the American Can Company and other corporations that had the effect of blaming individuals and discouraging questions about who profits from the production of disposable merchandise and its packaging.[33]

But let's return to the students sitting in our classrooms. If the question is: "How can we get them to raise their hands and wait to be called on rather than blurting out the answer?" then the question *isn't:* "Why does the teacher ask most of the questions in here—and unilaterally decide who gets to speak, and when?" If the question is: "What's the best way to teach kids self-discipline so they'll do their work?" then the question *isn't:* "Are these assignments, which feel like 'work,'[34] really worth doing? Do they promote deep thinking and excitement about learning, or are they just about memorizing facts and practicing skills by rote?" In other words, *to identify a lack of self-discipline as the problem is to focus our efforts on making children conform to a status quo that is left unexamined and is unlikely to change.* Each child, moreover, has been equipped with "a built-in supervisor," which may not be in his or her best interest but is enormously convenient for creating "a self-controlled—not just controlled—citizenry and work force."[35]

Not every objection, or piece of evidence, reviewed here will apply to every example of self-discipline. But it makes sense for us to take a closer look at the concept and the ways in which it's applied in our schools. Aside from its philosophical underpinnings and political impact, there are reasons to be skeptical about anything that might produce overcontrol. Some children who look like every adult's dream of a dedicated student may in reality be anxious, driven, and motivated by a perpetual need to feel better about themselves, rather than by anything resembling curiosity. In a word, they are workaholics in training.

On Marshmallows and Gender Differences: Rereading Self-Discipline Research

Four decades ago, in the Stanford University laboratory of Walter Mischel, preschool-age children were left alone in a room after having been told they could get a small treat (say, a marshmallow) by ringing a bell at any time to summon the experimenter—or, if they held out until he returned on his own, they could have a bigger treat (two marshmallows). As the results of this experiment are usually summarized, the children who were able to wait scored better on measures of cognitive and social skills about a decade later and also had higher SAT scores. The lesson is simple, as conservative commentators tell the story: We ought to focus less on "structural reforms" to improve education or reduce poverty, and look instead at traits possessed by individuals—specifically, the ability to exert good old-fashioned self-control.[36]

But the real story of these studies is a good deal more complicated. For starters, the causal relationship wasn't at all clear, as Mischel acknowledged. The ability to delay gratification might not have been responsible for the impressive qualities found ten years later; instead, both may have resulted from the same kind of home environment.[37]

Second, what mostly interested Mischel wasn't whether children could wait for a bigger treat—which, by the way, most of them could[38]—and whether waiters fared better in life than non-waiters, but how children go about trying to wait and which strategies help. It turned out that kids waited longer when they were distracted by a toy. What worked best wasn't "self-denial and grim determination" but doing something enjoyable while waiting so that self-control wasn't needed at all![39]

Third, the specifics of the situation—that is, the design of each experiment—were more important than the personality of a given child in predicting the outcome.[40] This is precisely the opposite of the usual lesson drawn from these studies, which is that self-control is a matter of individual character, which we ought to promote.

Fourth, even to the extent Mischel did look at stable individual characteristics, he was primarily concerned with "cognitive competencies"—strategies for how to think about (or stop thinking about) the goody—and how they're related to other skills that are measured down the road. In fact, those subsequent outcomes weren't associated with the ability to defer gratification, per se, but only with the ability to distract oneself when those distractions weren't provided by the experimenters.[41] And that ability was significantly correlated with plain old intelligence.[42]

Finally, most people who cite these experiments simply assume that it's better to take a bigger payoff later than a smaller payoff now. But is that always true? Mischel, for one, didn't think so. "The decision to delay or not to delay hinges, in part, on the individual's values and expectations with regard to the specific contingencies," he and his colleagues wrote. "In a given situation, therefore, postponing gratification may or may not be a wise or adaptive choice."[43]

If the conservative spin on Mischel's work is mostly attributable to how others have (mis)interpreted it, the same can't be said of a more recent study, where the researchers themselves are keen to blame underachievement on the "failure to exercise self-discipline." Angela Duckworth and Martin Seligman attracted considerable attention (in *Education Week*, the *New York Times*, and elsewhere) for their experiment, published in 2005 and 2006, purporting to show that self-discipline was a strong predictor of academic success, and that this trait explained why girls in their sample were more successful in school than boys.[44]

Once again, the conclusion is a lot more dubious once you look more closely. For one thing, all of the children in this study were eighth graders at an elite magnet school with competitive admissions, so it's not at all clear that the findings can be generalized to other populations or ages. For another thing, self-discipline was mostly assessed by how the students described themselves, or how their teachers and parents described them, rather than being based on something they actually did. The sole behavioral measure—making them choose either a dollar today or two dollars in a week—correlated weakly with the other measures and showed the smallest gender difference.

Most tellingly, though, the only beneficial effect of self-discipline was higher grades. Teachers gave more A's to the students who said, for example, that they put off doing what they enjoyed until they finished their homework. Suppose it had been discovered that students who nodded and smiled at everything their teacher said received higher grades. Would that argue for teaching kids to nod and smile more, or might it call into question the significance of grades as a variable? Or suppose it was discovered that self-discipline on the part of adults was associated with more positive evaluations from workplace supervisors. We'd have to conclude that employees who did what their bosses wanted, regardless of whether it was satisfying or sensible, elicited a favorable verdict from those same bosses. But so what?

We already know not only that grades suffer from low levels of validity and reliability but that students who are led to focus on grades tend to be less interested in what they're learning, more likely to think in a superficial fashion (and to retain information for a shorter time), and apt to choose the easiest possible task.[45] Moreover, there's some evidence that students with high grades are, on average, overly conformist and not particularly creative.[46] That students who are more self-disciplined get better grades, then, constitutes an endorsement of self-discipline only for people who don't understand that grades are a terrible marker for the educational qualities we care about. And if girls in our culture are socialized to control their impulses and do what they're told, is it really a good thing that they've absorbed that lesson well enough to be rewarded with high marks?

Notes

1. Jack Block, *Personality as an Affect-Processing System: Toward an Integrative Theory* (Mahway, NJ: Erlbaum, 2002), pp. 195, 8–9. Or, as a different psychologist puts it, "One person's lack of self-control is another person's impetus for a positive life change" (Laura A. King, "Who Is Regulating What and Why?" *Psychological Inquiry* 7 [1996]: 58).

2. "Our belief [is] that there is no true disadvantage of having too much self-control," Christopher Peterson and Martin Seligman wrote in their book *Character Strengths and Virtues* (New York: Oxford University Press, 2004), p. 515. June Tangney, Roy Baumeister, and Angie Luzio Boone similarly declared that "self-control is beneficial and adaptive in a linear fashion. We found no evidence that any psychological problems are linked to high self-control" (Tangney et al., "High Self-Control Predicts Good Adjustment, Less Pathology, Better Grades, and Interpersonal Success," *Journal of Personality* 72 [2004]: 296). This conclusion—based on questionnaire responses by a group of undergraduates—turns out to be a trifle misleading, if not disingenuous. First, it's supported by the fact that Tangney and her colleagues found an inverse relationship between self-control and negative emotions. Other research, however, has found that there's also an inverse

relationship between self-control and *positive* emotions. (See, for example, Darya L. Zabelina et al., "The Psychological Tradeoffs of Self-Control," *Personality and Individual Differences* 43 [2007]: 463–73.) Even if highly self-controlled people aren't always unhappy, they're also not particularly happy; their emotional life in general tends to be muted. Second, the self-control questionnaire used by Tangney and her colleagues "includes items reflective of an appropriate level of control and [of] undercontrol, but not overcontrol. It is therefore not surprising that the correlates of the scale do not indicate maladaptive consequences associated with very high levels of control" (Tera D. Letzring et al., "Ego-Control and Ego-Resiliency," *Journal of Research in Personality* 39 [2005]: 3). In other words, the clean bill of health they award to self-control was virtually predetermined by the design of their study. At the very end of their article, Tangney et al. concede that some people may be rigidly overcontrolled but then immediately try to define the problem out of existence: "Such overcontrolled individuals may be said to lack the ability to control their self-control" (Tangney et al., "High Self-Control Predicts Good Adjustment," p. 314).

3. The first sentence is from Joseph F. Rogus, "Promoting Self-Discipline: A Comprehensive Approach," *Theory Into Practice* 24 (1985): 271. The second is from a Web page of the Curriculum, Technology, and Education Reform program at the University of Illinois at Urbana-Champaign (http://wik .ed.uiuc.edu/index.php/Self-Discipline). Rogus's article appeared in a special issue of the journal *Theory into Practice* devoted entirely to the topic of self-discipline. Although it featured contributions by a wide range of educational theorists, including some with a distinctly humanistic orientation, none questioned the importance of self-discipline.

4. Letzring et al., "Ego-Control and Ego-Resiliency," p. 3.

5. Scott J. Dickman, "Functional and Dysfunctional Impulsivity," *Journal of Personality and Social Psychology* 58 (1990): 95.

6. Zabelina et al., "The Psychological Tradeoffs of Self-Control."

7. Daniel A. Weinberger and Gary E. Schwartz, "Distress and Restraint as Superordinate Dimensions of Self-Reported Adjustment," *Journal of Personality* 58 (1990): 381–417.

8. David C. Funder, "On the Pros and Cons of Delay of Gratification," *Psychological Inquiry* 9 (1998): 211. The studies to which he alludes are, respectively, Jonathan Shedler and Jack Block, "Adolescent Drug Use and Psychological Health," *American Psychologist* 45 (1990): 612–30; and Jack H. Block, Per E. Gjerde, and Jeanne H. Block, "Personality Antecedents of Depressive Tendencies in 18-Year-Olds," *Journal of Personality and Social Psychology* 60 (1991): 726–38.

9. For example, see Christine Halse, Anne Honey, and Desiree Boughtwood,

"The Paradox of Virtue: (Re)thinking Deviance, Anorexia, and Schooling," *Gender and Education* 19 (2007): 219–35.

10. This may explain why the data generally fail to show any academic benefit to assigning homework—which most students detest—particularly in elementary or middle school. (See Alfie Kohn, *The Homework Myth* [Cambridge, MA: Da Capo Press, 2006].) Remarkably, most people assume that students will somehow benefit from performing tasks they can't wait to be done with, as though their attitudes and goals were irrelevant to the outcome.

11. David Shapiro, *Neurotic Styles* (New York: Basic Books, 1965), p. 34.

12. Ibid., p. 44.

13. Funder, "On the Pros and Cons,"p. 211.

14. Regarding the way that "disinhibition [is] occasionally manifested by some overcontrolled personalities," see Block, *Personality*, p. 187.

15. Janet Polivy, "The Effects of Behavioral Inhibition," *Psychological Inquiry* 9 (1998): 183. She adds: "This is not to say that one should never inhibit one's natural response, as, for example, when anger makes one want to hurt another, or addiction makes one crave a cigarette." Rather, it means one should weigh the benefits and costs of inhibition in each circumstance— a moderate position that contrasts sharply with our society's tendency to endorse self-discipline across the board.

16. Funder, "On the Pros and Cons," p. 211. Walter Mischel, who conducted the so-called "marshmallow" experiments (see sidebar), put it this way: The inability to delay gratification may be a problem, but "the other extreme— excessive delay of gratification—also has its personal costs and can be disadvantageous. . . . Whether one should or should not delay gratification or 'exercise the will' in any particular choice is often anything but self-evident" ("From Good Intentions to Willpower," in *The Psychology of Action: Linking Cognition and Motivation to Behavior,* eds. Peter M. Gollwitzer and John A. Bargh [New York: Guilford, 1996], p. 198).

17. See, for example, King, "Who Is Regulating What and Why?"; and Alina Tugend, "Winners Never Quit? Well, Yes, They Do," *New York Times,* August 16, 2008, p. B-5, for data that challenge an unqualified endorsement of perseverance such as is offered by psychologist Angela Duckworth and her colleagues: "As educators and parents we should encourage children to work not only with intensity but also with stamina." That advice follows their report that perseverance contributed to higher grades and better performance at a spelling bee (Angela L. Duckworth et al., "Grit: Perseverance and Passion for Long-Term Goals," *Journal of Personality and Social Psychology* 92 [2007]; quotation on p. 1100). But such statistical associations mostly point up the limitations of these outcome measures as well as of

grit itself, a concept that ignores motivational factors (that is, *why* people persevere), thus conflating genuine passion for a task with a desperate need to prove one's competence, an inability to change course when appropriate, and so on.

18. Block, *Personality*, p. 130.

19. See, for example, my book *Punished by Rewards: The Trouble with Gold Stars, Incentive Plans, A's, Praise, and Other Bribes*, rev. ed. (Boston: Houghton Mifflin, 1999); and Edward L. Deci et al., "A Meta-Analytic Review of Experiments Examining the Effects of Extrinsic Rewards on Intrinsic Motivation," *Psychological Bulletin* 125 (1999): 627–68.

20. Richard M. Ryan, Scott Rigby, and Kristi King, "Two Types of Religious Internalization and Their Relations to Religious Orientations and Mental Health," *Journal of Personality and Social Psychology* 65 (1993): 587. This basic distinction has been explicated and refined in many other writings by Ryan, Deci, Robert J. Vallerand, James P. Connell, Richard Koestner, Luc Pelletier, and others. Most recently, it has been invoked in response to Roy Baumeister's claim that the capacity for self-control is "like a muscle," requiring energy and subject to being depleted—such that if you resist one sort of temptation, you'll have, at least temporarily, less capacity to resist another. The problem with this theory is its failure to distinguish "between self-regulation (i.e., autonomous regulation) and self-control (i.e., controlled regulation)." Ego depletion may indeed take place with the latter, but the former actually "maintains or enhances energy or vitality" (Richard M. Ryan and Edward L. Deci, "From Ego Depletion to Vitality," *Social and Personality Psychology Compass* 2 [2008]: 709, 711).

21. See, for example, Richard M. Ryan, James P. Connell, and Edward L. Deci, "A Motivational Analysis of Self-Determination and Self-Regulation in Education," in *Research on Motivation in Education*, vol. 2, eds. Carole Ames and Russell Ames (Orlando, FL: Academic Press, 1985); and Richard M. Ryan and Jerome Stiller, "The Social Contexts of Internalization: Parent and Teacher Influences on Autonomy, Motivation, and Learning," *Advances in Motivation and Achievement* 7 (1991): 115–49. The quotation is from the latter, p. 143.

22. David Brooks, "The Art of Growing Up," *New York Times*, June 6, 2008, p. A-23.

23. See Alfie Kohn, "How Not to Teach Values: A Critical Look at Character Education," *Phi Delta Kappan*, February 1997, pp. 429–39.

24. One educator based his defense of the need for self-discipline on "our natural egoism [that threatens to] lead us into 'a condition of warre one against another'"—as though Thomas Hobbes's dismal view of our species was universally accepted. This was followed by the astonishing assertion

that "social class differences appear to be largely a function of the ability to defer gratification" and the recommendation that we "connect the lower social classes to the middle classes who may provide role models for self-discipline" (Louis Goldman, "Mind, Character, and the Deferral of Gratification," *Educational Forum* 60 [1996]: 136, 137, 139). Notice that this article was published in 1996, not in 1896.

25. To whatever extent internalization or self-discipline *is* desired, this gentler approach—specifically, supporting children's autonomy and minimizing adult control—has consistently been shown to be more effective. (I reviewed some of the evidence in *Unconditional Parenting* [New York: Atria, 2005], especially in chapter 3.) Ironically, many of the same traditionalists who defend the value of self-control also promote a more authoritarian approach to parenting or teaching. In any case, my central point here is that we need to reconsider the goal, not merely the method.

26. "The older generation has complained about the lack of self-control among the younger generation for decades, if not centuries. The older generation of Vikings no doubt complained that the younger generation were getting soft and did not rape and pillage with the same dedication as in years gone by" (C. Peter Herman, "Thoughts of a Veteran of Self-Regulation Failure," *Psychological Inquiry* 7 [1996]: 46). The following rant, for example, is widely attributed to the Greek poet Hesiod, who lived about 2,700 years ago: "When I was young, we were taught to be discreet and respectful of elders, but the present youth are exceedingly [disrespectful] and impatient of restraint." Likewise, grade inflation, another manifestation of allegedly lower standards, was denounced at Harvard University in 1894, shortly after letter grades were introduced there.

27. George Lakoff, *Moral Politics: How Liberals and Conservatives Think*, 2nd ed. (Chicago: University of Chicago Press, 2002).

28. For a discussion of the relationship between obedience and self-control, see Block, *Personality*, especially pp. 195–96.

29. I'm thinking specifically of Roy Baumeister and his collaborator June Tangney, as well as Martin Seligman and Angela Duckworth, and, in a different academic neighborhood, criminologists Michael R. Gottfredson and Travis Hirschi, who argued that crime is simply due to a lack of self-control on the part of criminals. (For a critique of that theory, see *Out of Control: Assessing the General Theory of Crime*, ed. Erich Goode [Stanford, CA: Stanford University Press, 2008], particularly the chapter by Gilbert Geis entitled "Self-Control: A Hypercritical Assessment.")

30. I discussed the fundamental attribution error in an article about academic cheating, which is typically construed as a reflection of moral failure (one often attributed to a lack of self-control), even though researchers have

found that it is a predictable response to certain educational environments. See "Who's Cheating Whom?" which appears as chapter 5 of this volume.

31. Per-Olof H. Wikström and Kyle Treiber, "The Role of Self-Control in Crime Causation," *European Journal of Criminology* 4 (2007): 243, 251. Regarding delay of gratification, see Walter Mischel et al., "Cognitive and Attentional Mechanisms in Delay of Gratification," *Journal of Personality and Social Psychology* 21 (1972): 204–18.

32. For example, see CBS News, "Meet 'Generation Plastic,'" May 17, 2007, available at www.cbsnews.com/stories/2007/05/17/eveningnews/main2821916 .shtml.

33. See Heather Rogers, *Gone Tomorrow: The Hidden Life of Garbage* (New York: New Press, 2005).

34. See Alfie Kohn, "Students Don't 'Work,' They Learn: Our Use of Workplace Metaphors May Compromise the Essence of Schooling," *Education Week*, September 3, 1997, pp. 60, 43.

35. Samuel Bowles and Herbert Gintis, *Schooling in Capitalist America* (New York: Basic Books, 1976), p. 39. Perhaps it shouldn't be surprising that the conservative *National Review* published an essay strongly supporting homework because it teaches "personal responsibility and self-discipline. Homework is practice for life" (John D. Gartner, "Training for Life," January 22, 2001). But what aspect of life? The point evidently is not to train children to make meaningful decisions, or become part of a democratic society, or learn to think critically. Rather, what's being prescribed are lessons in doing whatever one is told.

36. For example, see David Brooks, "Marshmallows and Public Policy," *New York Times*, May 7, 2006, p. A-13.

37. Mischel, "From Good Intentions," p. 212.

38. A "remarkably consistent finding" in delay-of-gratification studies, at least those designed so that waiting yields a bigger reward, is that "most children and adolescents do manage to delay." In one such experiment, "83 out of the 104 subjects delayed the maximum number of times" (David C. Funder and Jack Block, "The Role of Ego-Control, Ego-Resiliency, and IQ in Delay of Gratification in Adolescence," *Journal of Personality and Social Psychology* 57 [1989]: 1048). This suggests either that complaints about the hedonism and self-indulgence of contemporary youth may be exaggerated or that these studies of self-control are so contrived that *all* of their findings are of dubious relevance to the real world.

39. Mischel, "From Good Intentions," 209.

40. Ibid., p. 212. See also Walter Mischel, Yuichi Shoda, and Philip K. Peake, "The Nature of Adolescent Competencies Predicted by Preschool Delay of Gratification," *Journal of Personality and Social Psychology* 54 (1988): 694.

41. Mischel, "From Good Intentions," p. 211.

42. Ibid., p. 214. This finding is interesting in light of the fact that other writers have treated self-discipline and intelligence as very different characteristics. (See, for example, the title of the first article in note 44.)

43. Yuichi Shoda, Walter Mischel, and Philip K. Peake, "Predicting Adolescent Cognitive and Self-Regulatory Competencies from Preschool Delay of Gratification," *Developmental Psychology* 26 (1990): 985. They add that the *ability* to put up with delay so one can make that choice is valuable, but of course this is different from arguing that the exercise of self-control in itself is beneficial.

44. Angela L. Duckworth and Martin E. P. Seligman, "Self-Discipline Outdoes IQ in Predicting Academic Performance of Adolescents," *Psychological Science* 16 (2005): 939–44; and Angela Lee Duckworth and Martin E. P. Seligman, "Self-Discipline Gives Girls the Edge," *Journal of Educational Psychology* 98 (2006): 198–208.

45. I've reviewed the evidence on grades in *Punished by Rewards* (Boston: Houghton Mifflin, 1993) and *The Schools Our Children Deserve* (Boston: Houghton Mifflin, 1999).

46. Consider one of the studies that Duckworth and Seligman cite to prove that self-discipline predicts academic performance (that is, high grades). It found that such performance "seemed as much a function of attention to details and the rules of the academic game as it was of intellectual talent." High-achieving students "were not particularly interested in ideas or in cultural or aesthetic pursuits. Moreover, they were not particularly tolerant or empathic; however, they did seem stable, pragmatic, and task-oriented, and lived in harmony with the rules and conventions of society. Finally, relative to students in general, these superior achievers seemed somewhat stodgy and unoriginal" (Robert Hogan and Daniel S. Weiss, "Personality Correlates of Superior Academic Achievement," *Journal of Counseling Psychology* 21 [1974]: 148).

19.   Cash Incentives Won't
Make Us Healthier

In its first salvo at reforming health care, Congress is reportedly considering legislation that would do two things: help employers to set up wellness programs and encourage the use of financial incentives to promote healthier living.

The first idea is terrific. The second one is terrible.

Programs that reward employees who lose weight or stop smoking are already fairly common. A National Business Group on Health (NBGH) survey found that 30 to 40 percent of companies now offer such incentives.

Some critics say this amounts to corporate intrusion into employees' private lives. But there's a more fundamental problem: Paying people to become healthy simply doesn't work, at least not in the long run. Regardless of whether the goal is to increase quality of life or hold down costs, incentives are mostly ineffective—and may even be counterproductive.

In 2007, the Center on Budget and Policy Priorities reported that "published research does not support the idea that financial incentives are effective at getting people to stop smoking." The following year, an academic review of the available data agreed: "Smokers may quit while they . . . receive rewards for quitting, but do no better than unassisted quitters once the rewards stop."

Likewise, an NBGH summary of weight-loss research in 2007 concluded that the promise of a reward may induce people to join a program but there is "no lasting effect" in terms of slimming down.

Have newer studies had better luck with incentives, as press reports suggest? Last December, researchers supposedly found that people lost more weight if paid to do so. But the small, poorly designed study showed no statistically significant difference at the final weigh-in. A study of incentives and smoking published earlier this year produced a similar discrepancy between breathless news accounts and unimpressive actual findings.

Originally published in *USA Today*, May 21, 2009

By contrast, three better-designed experiments—in which various kinds of training and support were provided for quitting smoking—discovered that the effectiveness of these interventions was *reduced* if a reward was offered for kicking the habit. In some cases, people promised money actually fared worse than those who weren't in a program at all! (For more details about all of this research, please see the Appendix to this chapter.)

If these results seem surprising, it may be because of how we tend to think about motivation—namely, as something that goes up when we're offered a dollar, an A, or a "Good job!" But psychologists now realize that there are different types of motivation—and the type matters more than the amount.

"Extrinsic" motivation (to get a reward or avoid a punishment) is much less effective than "intrinsic" (a commitment to doing something for its own sake). What's more, the two are often inversely related. Scores of studies confirm that the more we're rewarded for doing something—at work, at school, or at home—the more we're apt to lose interest in whatever we had to do to get the reward.

Thus, a study published in *Developmental Psychology* in 2008 showed, as did two previous experiments, that children who are rewarded for helping or sharing subsequently become *less* helpful. Similarly, the more that students are led to focus on getting good grades, the less interesting they come to find the learning itself. They also think less deeply on average than students who aren't graded.

Adjusting the size, type, or scheduling of the incentive doesn't help because the problem is with the outdated theory of motivation on which all rewards are based. Unfortunately, that psychological theory is still accepted by most economists—including those in the trendy field of behavioral economics—who, in turn, influence public policy.

Sure, bribes and threats can produce temporary compliance. Offer a reward to adults for going to the gym, or to children for picking up a book, and it may work—for awhile. But they come to think of themselves as extrinsically motivated, so when the reward is no longer available there's no reason to continue. Indeed, they may wind up less interested in exercising or reading than they were before.

Rewards have been called "sugar-coated control." We like the money—or the candy or the praise—but we resent being manipulated with it. Also, rewards are based only on observable behaviors. They ignore the *reasons* we may turn to food or cigarettes for solace.

"Smoking, drinking, overeating, or not exercising often represent coping strategies for some kind of underlying distress," Dr. Jonathan Robison, a health educator, observes. Incentive programs not only ignore those problems but may produce "a cycle of repeated failure."

Better answers: First, address people's motives and deeper concerns rather than just trying to change their behavior. Second, help people to get some control over their lives. Finally, build on their relationships with others to promote change. Couples and friends tend to lose weight together more effectively than do individuals.

Health can be a tough sell. But it's clearly something that incentives can't buy.

Appendix

Incentives and Health Promotion: What Do the Data Really Say?

My book *Punished by Rewards* reviews quite a number of studies showing that incentives tend to diminish people's interest (in whatever they were rewarded for doing) as well as the quality of their performance. But a fair amount of research dealing with health promotion—and, specifically, the effects of rewards on smoking cessation and weight loss—has been conducted since that book's publication. So when I was asked to speak at the annual conference sponsored by the *American Journal of Health Promotion* in 2009, I decided to collect and review the available studies, in part because, to my knowledge, no one else has ever done so. Here, then, is more information about the research to which I just alluded.

Smoking

Research reviews

1. Dyann M. Matson et al., "The Impact of Incentives and Competitions on Participation and Quit Rates in Worksite Smoking Cessation Programs," *American Journal of Health Promotion* 7 (1993): 270–80, 295.
   • Reviewed all available research from 1960s through early 1990s.
   • Most studies were found to be of very poor quality: Out of thirty, only eight had "an appropriate comparison group which allowed separation of the effects of incentives and competition from other program elements." And only three looked at effects after twelve months or more.
   • Of eight studies with an appropriate comparison group, only three even found greater *participation* in the program as a result of incentives. And "the research did not show incentives and competition enhancing long-term quit rates past 6 months."

2. Pat Redmond et al., "Can Incentives for Healthy Behavior Improve Health and Hold Down Medicaid Costs?" Center on Budget and Policy Priorities, June 2007.
   • "Published research does not support the idea that financial incentives are effective at getting people to stop smoking. Although financial rewards may prompt people to use self-help materials or even to quit for a short time, no research has shown that financial rewards produce improvement in the number of people who succeed in quitting smoking entirely."

3. Kate Cahill and Rafael Perera, "Competitions and Incentives for Smoking Cessation," *Cochrane Database of Systematic Reviews*, issue 3 (2008).
   • Looked for all rigorous controlled studies and found seventeen.
   • "None of the studies demonstrated significantly higher quit rates for the incentives group than for the control group beyond the six-month assessment. . . . Smokers may quit while they take part in

a competition or receive rewards for quitting, but do no better than unassisted quitters once the rewards stop."

Most recent study

Press accounts of a Philadelphia Veterans Administration study (Kevin G. Volpp et al., "A Randomized Controlled Trial of Financial Incentives for Smoking Cessation," *New England Journal of Medicine* 360 [February 12, 2009]: 699–709) claimed that a positive effect from incentives had finally been found.

But a careful reading of the study itself reveals the following:

• The study didn't evaluate any non-incentive interventions. Participants either received an incentive for quitting or were in the control group and received no help at all;

• The "primary endpoint" for judging the effect was at twelve months, even though rewards were still being paid at that point. (What matters is how people fare after the rewards have stopped);

• At fifteen or eighteen months, the quit rate for those receiving incentives was greater than for those in the control group, but it was still extremely low in absolute terms: below 10 percent;

• For those in the incentive group who did manage to quit after nine or twelve months, about one in three subjects started smoking again once another six months had passed. That relapse rate was actually higher than for those in the control group.

Better studies

What about studies that offered various types of intervention to help people quit, so that the effect of an incentive could be evaluated in conjunction with these cessation programs?

1. Dyann Matson Koffman et al., "The Impact of Including Incentives and Competition in a Workplace Smoking Cessation Program on Quit Rates," *American Journal of Health Promotion* 13 (1998): 105–11.

• A very large study at three worksites that featured a multicomponent program (a self-help package plus small-group support and monthly phone counseling)—with and without incentives. These incentives "were much larger and were provided over a longer period than in other controlled studies." Also evaluated was a contest among groups to see which had the best quit rate. Effects were evaluated at twelve months.

• Results: (a) no significant benefit from the incentive; (b) anecdotally, the contest was particularly counterproductive; and (c) in discussing what did seem to help, "counselors emphasized self-control and confidence building so that participants did not attribute their cessation to external factors such as incentives"—meaning that an effort had to be made to try to counteract the negative effects of using rewards.

2. Richard A. Windsor et al., "The Effectiveness of a Worksite Self-Help Smoking Cessation Program: A Randomized Trial," *Journal of Behavioral Medicine* 11 (1988): 407–21.

• Random assignment to four conditions featuring various combinations of different interventions: a self-help manual; skill training and "social enhancement"; and an incentive. Effects were evaluated at twelve months.

• Result: The incentive not only didn't help, but it reduced the effectiveness of other strategies.

3. Susan J. Curry et al., "Evaluation of Intrinsic and Extrinsic Motivation Interventions with a Self-Help Smoking Cessation Program," *Journal of Consulting and Clinical Psychology* 59 (1991): 318–24.

• Four conditions: personalized feedback (highlighting intrinsic reasons for quitting based on people's questionnaire responses), an incentive, both, and neither (control group).

• Results: Incentive recipients were more likely to return the first progress report, but they had worse long-term results than those who got the feedback with no incentive—and also did worse than those in the control group. Incentive recipients had higher relapse rates than those in the feedback *or* control group and were twice as likely to lie about quitting.

Weight Loss

Research review

National Business Group on Health's Institute on the Costs and Health Effects of Obesity, "Financial Incentives—Summary of the Current Evidence Base: What (and How) Incentives Work," 2007.

• Despite an obvious pro-incentive bias—the stated purpose of the report being to advise companies on how, not whether, to design incentive plans—the authors conclude with apparent reluctance that rewards at best can increase participation rates in a program and boost short-term compliance, but the evidence finds "no lasting effect" on weight loss (or smoking cessation).

Early studies

1. Richard A. Dienstbier and Gary K. Leak, "Overjustification and Weight Loss: The Effects of Monetary Reward," paper presented at the annual convention of the American Psychological Association, 1976.

• Very small study. Subjects weighed twice a week. Only two conditions: incentive and control group.

• Incentive recipients made more progress at the beginning, but after incentives stopped, control subjects lost an average of 3.5 pounds, while incentive subjects *gained* 6.1 pounds.

2. F. Matthew Kramer et al., "Maintenance of Successful Weight Loss over 1 Year," *Behavior Therapy* 17 (1986): 295–301.

• At twelve-month follow-up: "The principal hypothesis, that subjects entering into financial contracts for attending skills training sessions or for maintaining post-treatment weight would show better maintenance one year after successful weight loss than subjects receiving no maintenance support, was not confirmed."

The only significant difference: Many incentive recipients failed to show up for the final weigh-in.

Most recent study

Another report using the same Philadelphia V. A. study mentioned above (Kevin G. Volpp et al., "Financial Incentive-Based Approaches for Weight Loss," *Journal of the American Medical Association* 300 [December 10, 2008]: 2631–37) was, like the smoking cessation study, widely described as having demonstrated the effectiveness of incentives. However,

• The study was very small (only nineteen people in each condition, almost all of whom were men) and, again, did not evaluate any non-incentive interventions; subjects received only incentives or nothing;

• Only subjects in the reward condition were weighed daily, so any positive effect that might have been found could well have been from the motivation of the expected weighing rather than from the reward;

• News accounts mentioned early results favoring those who received incentives but failed to mention the bottom line: At the final follow-up, incentives provided no significant benefit.

Credits

Each essay in this volume is copyrighted in the year of its publication by Alfie Kohn. Reprint requests should be directed to the author in care of www.alfiekohn.org.

Chapter 1, "Progressive Education," was originally published in *Independent School*, Spring 2008, pp. 19–28.

Chapter 2, "Challenging Students—and How to Have More of Them," was originally published in *Phi Delta Kappan*, November 2004, pp. 184–94.

Chapter 3, "Getting Hit on the Head Lessons," was originally published in *Education Week*, September 7, 2005, pp. 52, 46–47.

Chapter 4, "It's Not What We Teach; It's What They Learn," was originally published in *Education Week*, September 10, 2008, pp. 32, 26.

Chapter 5, "Who's Cheating Whom?" was originally published in *Phi Delta Kappan*, October 2007, pp. 89–97.

Chapter 6, "How to Create Nonreaders," was originally published in *English Journal*, September 2010, pp. 16–22.

Chapter 7, "The Trouble with Rubrics," was originally published in *English Journal*, March 2006, pp. 12–15. This essay is adapted from the foreword to *Rethinking Rubrics in Writing Assessment*, by Maja Wilson (Portsmouth, NH: Heinemann, 2006).

Chapter 8, "The Value of Negative Learning," was originally published in *Education Week*, September 16, 2009, pp. 40, 23. This essay is adapted from the foreword to *Turning Points,* an anthology published by the Alternative Education Research Organization.

Chapter 9, "Unconditional Teaching," was originally published in *Educational Leadership,* September 2005, pp. 20–24.

Chapter 10, "Safety from the Inside Out," was originally published in *Educational Horizons,* Fall 2004, pp. 33–41.

Chapter 11, "Bad Signs," was originally published in *Kappa Delta Pi Record,* Fall 2010, pp. 4–9.

Chapter 12, "Feel-Bad Education," was originally published in *Education Week,* September 15, 2004, pp. 44, 36.

Chapter 13, "Against 'Competitiveness,'" was originally published in *Education Week,* September 19, 2007, pp. 32, 26.

Chapter 14, "When Twenty-First-Century Schooling Just Isn't Good Enough: A Modest Proposal," was originally published in *District Administration,* February 2009, pp. 38–39.

Chapter 15, "Debunking the Case for National Standards," was originally published in *Education Week,* January 14, 2010, pp. 28, 30. This is a slightly expanded version of the article published in *Education Week*'s annual "Quality Counts" issue.

Chapter 16, "Atrocious Advice from Supernanny," was originally published in the *Nation,* May 23, 2005, pp. 8, 10. This is a slightly expanded version of the published article, which was titled "Supernanny State."

Chapter 17, "Parental Love with Strings Attached," was originally published in the *New York Times,* September 15, 2009, p. D-5. This is a slightly expanded version of the published article, which was titled "When a Parent's 'I Love You' Means 'Do as I Say.'"

Chapter 18, "Why Self-Discipline Is Overrated," was originally published in *Phi Delta Kappan,* November 2008, pp. 168–76.

Chapter 19, "Cash Incentives Won't Make Us Healthier," was originally published in *USA Today,* May 21, 2009, p. 11-A. This is an expanded version of the published article.

Index